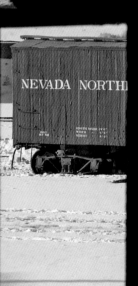

NEVADA NORTHERN

Railroad
Rolling Stock
By Steve Barry

Voyageur Press

First published in 2008 by Voyageur Press, an imprint of MBI Publishing Company, 400 First Avenue North, Suite 300, Minneapolis, MN 55401 USA

Voyageur Press titles are also available at discounts in bulk quantity for industrial or sales-promotional use. For details write to Special Sales Manager at MBI Publishing Company, 400 First Avenue North, Suite 300, Minneapolis, MN 55401 USA.

To find out more about our books, visit us online at www.voyageurpress.com.

Editor: Dennis Pernu
Designer: Danielle Smith
Printed in China

Library of Congress Cataloging-in-Publication Data

Barry, Steve.
  Railroad rolling stock / Steve Barry.
      p. cm.
  Includes index.
  ISBN 978-0-7603-3260-3 (sb : alk. paper)
  1. Railroads—Rolling-stock. I. Title.
  TF375.B37 2008
  625.2—dc22
                                        2008023040

Front cover (main): Hopper cars gather in Bluefield, Virginia, on the Norfolk & Western. Long strings of coal hoppers head from here to tidewater at Norfolk for export. While railroading has undergone many changes since this photo was taken in the early 1980s, with intermodal trains replacing merchandise freights on the main lines, Appalachia still remains a stronghold for long strings of hoppers.

Frontispiece: Looking out the window of a railroad's general offices, a lonely boxcar represents the lifeblood of the line. That boxcar will carry the goods that generate the revenue that pays the employees and earns a profit. Just a boxcar? Hardly.

Title pages: After a steady decline from the 1940s to the 1970s, the passenger train is making a remarkable twenty-first-century comeback. Modern bi-level commuter cars carry homeward-bound businesspeople to and from cities such as San Jose, California. This Altamont Commuter Express train will terminate in Stockton.

Author Bio

Steve Barry has had a lifelong interest in trains, beginning as a child in southern New Jersey. He graduated from Rutgers University in 1979 and has been contributing to the rail-hobby press for more than 20 years. In 1996 he left the accounting profession to join the staff of *Railfan & Railroad*.

Steve will photograph anything on rails, and when not shooting or writing, he can be found in front of the TV watching *Star Trek* or NFL football. Steve and his wife reside in Newton, New Jersey, with numerous dogs and cats. This is Steve's second book for MBI/Voyageur Press, following *Rail Power* (1996).

Contents

Introduction

Introduction

One inescapable truth of life is "the more work you do, the less you are appreciated." The same holds true in the world of railroad rolling stock. While the locomotive has always captured the attention of poets, songwriters, and photographers, the cars behind the locomotive often are ignored (especially freight cars; passenger cars have received a little more attention).

Walk through any major railroad museum and you'll find proof of this. Most museums have several locomotives. Small yard engines share space with mammoth freight engines and high-drivered passenger power. You'll also find cabooses in abundance at museums, but cabooses were little more than rolling offices in regular service.

Passenger cars also are sometimes well-represented, but are usually extraordinary examples. Lush private observation cars used by the rich and famous are lovingly restored, and museums often feature a dining car display, complete with china carefully set on the tables. But the working cars—the coaches and sleeping cars that made up 90 percent of the passenger-car fleet—are in short supply. Some museums and most tourist railroads haul passengers with restored coaches, but usually this is more out of necessity than historical preservation.

The freight car gets even less notice in museums. The battered boxcars that have hauled everything from flour to auto parts, their sides dinged and dented, are off in the weeds behind the museum, used for storage. Hopper cars that hauled millions of tons of coal are nowhere to be seen. The same is true for gondolas, tank cars, and flatcars.

Freight cars predate locomotives by several decades. The first horse-hauled cars appeared in the 1700s when rails were first laid. Car wheels on wood rails had less resistance than car wheels on dirt, allowing the equine power to pull heavier loads. By the time steam locomotives finally caught on in the 1830s, the standard freight car was a short body riding on a four-wheel truck (two axles fairly close to each other). By the 1840s the axles were separated by a longer frame, resulting in two single-axle trucks under each car. Soon, each of those trucks became four-wheel sets, creating the first eight-wheel, two-truck freight car, the design that has dominated ever since. While the first freight cars could carry about five tons (10,000 pounds), capacity grew as track was improved and locomotives became more powerful. By the end of the nineteenth century, car capacity had grown to 40 tons (80,000 pounds). Today's freight cars, on average, carry about 110 tons (220,000 pounds).

Freight cars are designed to be as light, yet as strong as possible. The lighter the car, the more revenue-generating material can be placed in it. Steel has remained the standard into the twenty-first century, although there have been experiments (some successful) in the use of aluminum.

The first passenger cars appeared in the 1830s and were little more than stagecoaches mounted on a four-wheel truck. Extending the car and mounting it on two trucks provided a smoother ride and increased capacity. The basic design that has remained to this day—a center aisle with seats on each side—soon became the standard. Weight issues were more important than passenger comfort, however, so these early cars provided little leg room and no amenities. From the 1840s through the 1860s, items such as toilet closets, lamps, coal stoves, and clerestory roofs for better lighting and air circulation were added and passenger cars approached a weight of 10 tons.

After the Civil War, railroads took pride in their passenger cars, using the finest wood and painting and paneling the interiors. In the twentieth century, steel cars took over and specialized cars such as diners and sleepers made long-distance travel more comfortable.

So you can see that the rich history of railroad rolling stock closely parallels that of the locomotive, yet has gone largely underappreciated. Remember, however, that without the lowly boxcar, tank car, flatcar, coach, caboose, and others, all those rock star locomotives would have nothing to do!

Previous pages: Branch lines have connected the small towns of North America since the mid-nineteenth century. A small locomotive pulling a string of wooden boxcars makes up the typical local freight, the only connection to the outside world for many a village. The latest goods ordered from the Sears catalog come in, while the town's produce or manufactured products leave.

Chapter 1
Rolling Stock and the Railroads

Rolling Stock and the Railroads

The first railroad chartered in the United States was the Baltimore & Ohio, formed in 1827. Like most early railroads, it was constructed to move goods from the interior to the East Coast—business that was being handled by canals. Thus, the B&O pushed westward to the Ohio River from Baltimore, with its first rolling stock consisting of boxcars and flatcars. Reaching the West Virginia mountains, the B&O was soon purchasing hopper cars to move "black diamonds."

Tapping into the same markets was the Chesapeake & Ohio, with a history dating to the 1830s. It was developed to bring coal from Virginia's mines, traffic that was primarily handled on the James River prior to the railroad. Eventually, both the B&O and C&O became components of the Chessie System and, ultimately, today's CSX Transportation.

Other heritage components of CSX include the lines that were merged into the Seaboard System in the 1980s. The Atlantic Coast Line and Seaboard Air Line competed in shipping goods (primarily fresh produce) from Florida to the Northeast. As such, you were far more likely to find refrigerator cars and boxcars than hopper cars on these two roads. Today, CSX competes with highways for much of this traffic, and the former ACL and SAL see long trains of piggyback service.

The other big railroad serving the eastern United States in the twenty-first century is Norfolk Southern, which, like CSX, was formed from coal and perishable haulers. The Norfolk & Western was a symbol of the coal industry, with some of the most powerful steam locomotives ever built pulling long, black trains of hoppers. The Southern Railway epitomized the south, hauling goods from New Orleans and Atlanta.

Like the East, the western United States is also served by two large railroads. Union Pacific was a part of the first transcontinental railroad. Passenger service was a driving force in building the UP, and its completion cut travel time from the Mississippi River to the Pacific from six months to one week.

Meanwhile, the Southern Pacific expanded into what is now the Los Angeles Basin. The development of the refrigerator car—allowing perishables grown in warm climates during the winter months to be shipped to New York markets—became crucial to the SP's development. Trains of orange reefers (most of them owned by private shipping companies such as Pacific Fruit Express) were common into the 1950s.

The last major U.S. railroad is BNSF Railway, which to a large extent brackets the Union Pacific across the West. Across the Southwest are the lines of the former Atchison, Topeka & Santa Fe, a railroad that prided itself on premier passenger trains and fast, reliable freight service. Stack trains have become the staple of these lines. Meanwhile, the lines across the northern United States, primarily of Great Northern and Northern Pacific heritage, have also seen a rise in stack-train traffic, driven by goods arriving from Asia through Seattle and Tacoma, Washington. At one time, the GN and NP were primarily boxcar routes, and like most boxcar routes they lost a lot of their business to the highways before it came back to the tracks as intermodal traffic.

Canada's rolling stock largely reflects the open spaces of that country. Both of the nations's major railroads—Canadian National and Canadian Pacific—were large users of boxcars and covered hoppers to move grain eastward from the prairies. Meanwhile, boxcars worked the other direction, bringing goods from Canada's manufacturing centers to consumers in the West.

While freight car builders have busily evolved cars since the beginning of railroad history, passenger car builders have been limited by the very nature of the "commodity" hauled: people. When Amtrak purchased its two major fleets of cars, it turned to two historic builders. The Budd Company provided Amfleet cars, which remain the backbone of the railroad's Northeast operations some 30 years after they were built. Pullman-Standard, the company that was synonymous with passenger car construction for over a century, modernized Amtrak's long-distance trains. In Canada, VIA Rail opted for rebuilt Budd stainless-steel cars on its long-distance passenger trains. Corridor trains in the East were upgraded with matched locomotive and car sets from Bombardier.

Every railroad has a unique history, and its rolling stock is both a window on its past and a mirror on its personality in the present.

Previous pages: The face of modern railroading is the stack train. As goods have poured into North America from Asia, containers stacked two high ride well cars and carry goods inland and cross-country from Pacific ports. Most of the containers are riding their second mode of transportation on the rails, having arrived by ship; they'll finish their journey behind a truck on the highway.

Above: With lines extending deep into Appalachia, CSX has a need for thousands of hopper cars. Coal makes up over a quarter of all the railroad's car loadings, with more than 130 mines along its route. On the other end of the delivery cycle, hopper cars full of coal are delivered to more than 100 power plants. Virtually all coal is handled in unit trains, with the type of hopper car dictated by the customer's unloading technique—some unload the coal through the bottom of the car, while others rotate the entire car upside down for unloading.

Right: A variety of cars can be seen in this train leaving the New York metropolitan region. Just behind the locomotives are a mix of covered hopper cars and boxcars, while a flatcar can be seen farther back in the consist. Mixed merchandise still makes up a substantial portion of CSX freight traffic.

Most container traffic comes from Asia to a North American port on the Pacific. It then travels across the continent in container trains and is unloaded at eastern population centers. But where do all those empty containers go? A fresh set of container wells have arrived in northern New Jersey. Containers will be unloaded and added to the pile.

CSX serves the timber industry of the southeastern United States, carrying large volumes of woodchips from the timber mills to paper mills. Tall open-top hopper cars are used to transport the chips. These cars generally move in mixed merchandise freights, as the volume of chips required by a paper mill usually doesn't warrant the operation of a unit train.

CSX runs long strings of autoracks between the Midwest and East Coast, utilizing more than 12,000 multilevel flatcars. Of all the automobiles and light trucks produced in the United States, about one-third ride CSX rails at some point in their trip to the dealer or export terminal. Autoracks make up about 13 percent of the entire CSX freight car fleet.

One of the hottest trains on CSX (in terms of timekeeping) is one of the coldest (in terms of contents). Tropicana orange juice leaves the packaging plant in Bradenton, Florida, and heads northward in company-owned refrigerator cars to a distribution center in New Jersey. The orange consist makes its arrival in metropolitan New York in the early morning.

Norfolk Southern owns or leases 95,000 freight cars for its 20,000-mile system that blankets the eastern United States. Autoracks haul new automobiles from Midwest manufacturing plants to ports near New York City for export. Automobiles account for about 10 percent of the railroad's traffic.

Above: If one major railroad can be identified with one commodity, it's Norfolk Southern. Predecessor Norfolk & Western reached deep into the Appalachia coalfields, especially in West Virginia, to move millions of tons of black diamonds in long trains of black hopper cars.

Left: Norfolk Southern shuttles intermodal containers to the busy Florida market, handing off strings of well cars to Florida East Coast in Jacksonville. Intermodal traffic accounts for about 20 percent of NS's annual revenues; by comparison, coal accounts for 25 percent. NS uses some 11,000 leased piggyback flats and container well cars.

Right: Triple Crown offers RoadRailer service to the eastern United States and Canada. Norfolk Southern moves the bulk of Triple Crown's traffic in the East, while BNSF Railway serves Texas. Trains move to 12 hubs, where they are broken apart; individual trailers are then hauled over the highways to their final destinations.

Above: When Norfolk Southern annexed former Conrail lines in 1999, it added even more coal traffic. Western Pennsylvania's coalfields have seen long processions of conventional hopper cars emerge from the Allegheny Mountains. Domestic power plants are the primary consumer of Pennsylvania coal, but much of the coal is also sent for export.

While open hopper cars predominate on Norfolk Southern, the railroad also hauls a lot of covered hopper cars. NS owns nearly 9,000 covered hoppers, with another 3,000 leased. By comparison, the railroad owns 18,000 conventional open hopper cars, with another 39,000 gondolas, most of which are high-sided, rotary-dump coal cars.

A Union Pacific locomotive with a string of empty covered hopper cars in tow fights traffic in Lodi, California. The cars have just left the town's General Mills plant, where the grain they carried will be turned into breakfast cereals. Four cars is a fairly typical delivery to provide for the needs of the plant.

Left: Autorack trains are fairly common on the Union Pacific, whose 32,000 route miles cover the western United States. Although General Motors is the railroad's second-largest shipper, Union Pacific owns few autorack cars; most are owned by TTX (formerly Trailer Train Company), a car leasing company owned jointly by the major North American railroads.

Above: Union Pacific's largest customer is APL Limited, a steamship company that brings containers into Pacific ports—primarily Long Beach and Los Angeles. UP moves the containers east in long stack trains. Containers can be stacked two high in well cars, but this train only has single-high containers.

Above: In the 1990s, Southern Pacific (and later Union Pacific) operated the "Tank Train" in California to transport crude oil. The cars were connected by piping in sets of 12, allowing multiple cars to be unloaded from one position. The upside was that trains could be loaded faster and with less spillage. The downside was that if one car needed to be repaired, it took the other 11 interconnected cars out of service.

Opposite top: It isn't too difficult to tell that this train passing through the Oregon Cascades originated somewhere in the Pacific Northwest. Center-beam flatcars and boxcars indicate that this train serves the region's timber industry. The flatcars back in the train are carrying board lumber; the boxcars could contain lumber or paper products.

Opposite bottom: Old-time railroading meets new on UP's former Chicago & North Western main line in DeKalb, Illinois. A string of piggyback trailers, the modern face of railroading, passes under a coaling tower that provided steam locomotives with coal in a bygone time. Some 50 trains a day pass over this piece of Union Pacific.

Above: Like its predecessor Burlington Northern, BNSF Railway serves the busy ports of Seattle and Tacoma, Washington. Train after train of stack cars head east from here, carrying containers to be unloaded at eastern ports. The average BNSF intermodal train replaces 260 trucks on the highway.

Opposite top: If you want to see container trains, then BNSF's former Santa Fe transcontinental line between Chicago and California is the place to go. More than five million containers and trailers move on the line's piggyback and well cars. During the Christmas rush, some five million packages will ride in these cars—and that's just for UPS.

Opposite bottom: Autumn brings the grain rush and unit trains of covered hoppers to the western United States. BNSF carries grain from the Dakotas to Pacific ports, shipping enough grain annually to provide 900 million people with a year's supply of bread. About 50 percent of BNSF's covered hoppers carry grain bound for export.

Right: BNSF Railway (and predecessor Burlington Northern) reach deep into the Powder River Basin of Montana and Wyoming to tap the large, easy-to-reach coal deposits that feed power plants across the United States. BNSF employs more than 13,000 high-side gondolas and 11,000 conventional hopper cars to transport coal.

Above: The Chicago, Burlington & Quincy was the first railroad to order bi-level gallery-style passenger cars for service in the Chicago area, with the first cars arriving in 1950. Even after Metra took over Chicagoland commuter services, CB&Q successor Burlington Northern continued to operate the gallery cars over the "raceway" to Aurora.

Maintaining a railroad requires a variety of rolling stock, as this BNSF train displays. A support boxcar trails the locomotives, followed by machinery for replacing rails and ties. A long string of flatcars carry lengths of welded rail, with each rail riding several cars. The rail is surprisingly flexible, bending as the train rounds curves.

Above: The port of Vancouver is the busiest in Canada, keeping the country's two transcontinental railroads busy. Their long trip over the Rocky Mountains complete, a long train of containers on the Canadian National at Ashcroft, British Columbia, heads back to Vancouver for export.

Opposite bottom: While it may seem odd that a Canadian railroad serves the Gulf Coast, CN's takeover of the Illinois Central in 1998 allowed for exactly that. A train heading north through the Louisiana swamplands contains tank cars carrying petroleum products from the many refineries that surround New Orleans.

Above: Like their U.S. counterparts, Canadian railroads operated passenger trains until those operations were nationalized. In Canada, VIA Rail took over passenger operations in 1976. Just after VIA's takeover, a passenger train still looking very much as it did under Canadian National passes through Bayview Junction 40 miles west of Toronto. The passenger train has lightweight Tempo cars, while a caboose marks the end of a passing freight train.

Right: The nature of modern railroading is demonstrated in a meet between unit trains on the Canadian National: A long line of intermodal cars head east from Vancouver, while a unit train of covered hoppers heads west to get ready for the wheat rush. CPR owns 3,000 covered hoppers and leases an additional 23,000.

Above: Serving the Canadian forest industry, CPR handles paper products in boxcars. At one time, boxcars were the workhorse car of railroading, but specialization of cars for specific purposes and the containerization of goods have reduced its role. Once the most common car in a freight train, boxcars are now outnumbered by autoracks, intermodal cars, and all types of hopper cars.

To transport containers from the Pacific Coast, Canadian Pacific owns 1,000 well cars and leases another 5,500 from TTX. The CPR fleet was initially made up of single-well cars, along with articulated three-well and five-well sets. As part of its modernization, the railroad is replacing multi-well cars with singles, which gives better utilization.

Above: Kansas City Southern utilizes intermodal cars for its premium services out of Kansas City. Trains depart for Dallas with goods for eastern Texas, and to Laredo with Mexico-bound commerce. A half-million containers and trailers ride the KCS each year. Like most railroads, KCS leases the bulk of its intermodal cars from companies like TTX.

Opposite top: The additions atop the sides of these hopper cars indicate that they are for carrying light crushed rock, such as limestone. Railroads are large users of crushed rock, which serves as ballast along the right-of-way. Unfortunately for this train, crushed rock is not a time-sensitive commodity, and the time it takes to complete its journey will be extended as it takes to sidings to allow higher-priority freights to pass.

Opposite bottom: Kansas City Southern is the only major North American railroad with sister railroads in both the United States and Mexico. The result is a lot of mixed-merchandise trains moving bulk commodities between the two countries. On KCS, boxcars and covered hoppers are more common than intermodal traffic.

Above: Short ore cars, designed for handling heavy bulk loads, carry copper ore in Arizona. Originally built by Kennecott Copper, the now-independent Copper Basin Railway moves about 100,000 cars of ore each year between the mine and smelter. Outbound finished copper was moved in open gondolas, but theft has moved most copper shipments to the highways.

Right: The Cartier Railway in Quebec hauls iron ore for its owner, Quebec Cartier Mining, using 500 short open-top ore cars on a 240-mile route from the mines to the processor. These cars unload through bottom hatches. During peak times they run roundtrips almost continuously on a 26-hour cycle.

A string of tank cars crosses the Newport River at Morehead City, North Carolina, on the Beaufort & Morehead Railway. The tank cars are empty but will soon be filled with highly flammable aviation fuel at a transloading facility on Radio Island. The tank cars will be dispersed to military installations throughout the Southeast.

The Indiana Harbor Belt serves two functions. One is to move traffic between railroads in the busy Chicago terminal area. The other is to serve the steel mills east of Chicago. Flatcars carrying steel coils make their way around Chicagoland on the IHB, heading for the major railroads to be shipped throughout the country.

Left: One-customer short-line railroads live and die by conditions out of their control. Perhaps the most fragile existence is endured by a railroad linked to the timber and paper industry. Located in remote areas where the mill is the only customer, railroads like the Quebec Central may ship carloads of woodchips one day, only to discover that the mill has decided to close the next, resulting in an almost immediate shutdown of the line.

Above: ON Rail (originally Ontario Northland) serves remote areas in Canada's second-largest province. The town of Mosinee has no roads leading to it, so everything goes in by rail. In this "mixed train," we see intermodal trailers carrying perishables, automobiles, and trucks on flatcars; boxcars with assorted goods; and passenger cars at the rear.

Serving Industry

Railroads need customers to survive, and customers need railroads to ship their goods. The move by the United States from an agrarian nation to an industrial power was driven by these two intertwined needs.

To serve customers' needs, railroads have to provide the proper rolling stock. Thus, many specialized cars grew from what industry demanded. The coal industry needed hopper cars—lots of them—to move black diamonds from the Appalachian coalfields and Pennsylvania's anthracite region to East Coast cities. California's reputation as the nation's food supplier grew when refrigerated cars could carry produce to areas where crops didn't grow in the winter months. Grain needed to be distributed from the fields of Saskatchewan and Manitoba to make bread for Canada's cities. Thus, the railroads amassed large fleets of hopper cars, refrigerator cars, and covered hoppers. The rolling stock seen in a freight train was dictated by customer needs. The relationship between railroads and industry truly is a symbiotic one.

Some industries require specialized rolling stock for use on a local level. One prime example is the steel industry. While typical freight cars such as flatcars and gondolas could be used for shipping finished steel, mills require raw material to be handled by rail as well. Thus, bottle cars were developed to carry molten steel from the blast furnaces.

The timber industry also requires its own special cars. While conventional boxcars and flatcars have long carried lumber and paper products from the mill to the world, getting the timber to the mill requires specialized rolling stock. Rough track was laid into the forests and small locomotives pushed skeleton cars full of logs back to the mill. But getting those logs to the skeleton cars required a piece of rail equipment known as a "skidder." A skidder looks a lot like a crane, but its boom reaches much higher. From the boom, cables could be stretched a mile from the tracks. Logs were then attached to these cables and dragged to the railroad for loading. The timber industry also made use of camp cars, as lumberjacks often lived in the woods for a week at a time.

Industry influenced the evolution of the railcar as well. Boxcars grew bigger to accommodate the growing demand for automobiles, and eventually flatcars sprouted racks to carry Detroit's products even more efficiently. Boxcars were also used to transport grain, but the covered hopper was developed to speed loading and unloading. Coal was once loaded one car at a time and delivered to customers one car at a time. But as coal mines grew and power plants demanded thousands of tons of coal a day, the size of hopper cars grew accordingly; the cars not only became larger, they became lighter so more of the weight on the wheels could be used for coal.

Not all freight trains look alike. If you know what to look for, you can often guess where a train came from and where it's going. If you see a lot of lumber in center-beam flatcars heading through California, for instance, you can guess the train came from the Pacific Northwest's forests and is heading to feed housing in Las Vegas or Phoenix.

A closer look at the reporting marks on the car—the initials of the railroad that owns the car—and you can further guess if the lumber is coming from Washington State or even Canada.

The makeup and mix of freight trains changes with the flow of industry, as well. As the dog days of summer come to a close, you start seeing more covered hopper cars in consists as the grain rush begins. The number of autoracks seen on any given day is influenced by the output of the auto plants. And stack train traffic is heaviest in October when goods for Christmas are being imported from Asia. No two days on the railroad are ever the same.

Thus, railroads aren't an industry unto themselves. Their success is tied to the success of their customers, and that means they have to meet the needs of those customers. Rolling stock is not something the railroads purchase randomly—every car is bought to meet a need.

Previous pages: When demand is great enough, fleets of special-service cars are built to meet the needs of industries. Iron ore, being too heavy to ride in a conventional hopper car, requires shorter cars to carry more weight over the axles. Ore cars generally don't wander very far; usually they are used to shuttle ore from the mine to a nearby processor.

Hopper cars can be found in abundance around steel mills, used to transport coal and coke used in the steel-making process. Sometimes iron ore arrives via hopper cars, albeit hoppers that are only partially full, as they were not designed to carry dense loads. Ores usually are transported in smaller specialized cars called jennies.

Above: The gondola is the poor stepchild of the steel mill. Scrap metal coming into the mill is unceremoniously dropped into the car's open top, and the constant shuffling in the industrial environment always results in dings and dents. Heavy steel slabs are dropped into the cars for shipment out, resulting in still more dents.

Left: When hard times hit the U.S. steel industry, the railroads adapted. This Bethlehem Steel mill yard has been reused as a RoadRailer terminal. Long strings of hopper cars have been replaced by autoracks.

Right: Independent coal load-outs, where long unit trains of hopper cars or coal gondolas are filled, still dot the countryside in Appalachia, Ohio, and Indiana. Flood loading is now the most common way to fill an entire train, with the train moving at a slow, steady speed while the coal fills the hoppers. An entire train can be loaded in a couple of hours.

Above: Towering coal silos stand over the Powder River Basin in Wyoming and Montana, where Union Pacific and BNSF Railway move 50 trains a day. Lightweight aluminum coal hoppers (lighter hoppers can carry more coal) are the workhorses of the basin. Conventional bottom-dump hoppers and top-unloading rotary cars can be found in strings of 100-plus cars at the more than one dozen mines in the region.

Prior to the era of flood-loading hopper cars in long strings, the typical coal load-out was a tipple with individual hopper cars positioned to receive the coal. During this era, a few or even single steel hoppers were mixed into a general merchandise freight. In many areas of the country, steel hoppers have been supplanted by aluminum cars and bulk-loading has replaced the tipple.

Above: Woodchips are the first stage in the conversion of timber into paper. Timber mills chop the raw timber into small chips which are then placed in open hopper cars for transporting to paper mills. The chips are light, so a large volume can be carried in each hopper. Woodchip cars are easily identifiable—they are as long as hopper cars used for minerals, but are much taller.

Opposite top: Boxcars are used to transport the final products out of a paper mill. Rolls of paper leave the mill destined to become newspapers, magazines, napkins, and towels. It's difficult to miss a paper mill town, smoke rising in the air, boxcars sitting in the nearby yard, and a certain aroma in the air. Many paper mills employ their own diesel locomotives to handle the constant shuffling of cars.

Opposite bottom: Logging railroads have snaked deep into the forests of the South and Pacific Northwest. Logs are brought out on flatcars that are not much more than frames on trucks, some equipped with side stakes. Looking somewhat like an arachnid on its back, a car with stakes is called a spider car by some railroaders. Cars without stakes are often referred to as skeleton cars.

Grain mills, such as this one in Mason City, Iowa, need a constant supply of covered hopper cars to ship products out. Inbound grain generally comes from the fields to the elevators by truck, while trains of covered hoppers disperse the grain to bakeries, cereal manufacturers, breweries, and the like.

Times have changed on the Canadian prairies, where small grain elevators were once served by boxcars. Covered hoppers, many owned by the Canadian or provincial governments, replaced the boxcars. Now, high through-put concrete silos are replacing the wooden elevators. Long trains of covered hoppers still appear every autumn, though.

Once, the grain loaded at elevators would ultimately be distributed to feed mills in small towns across North America. The local feed mill has vanished from many communities, as small farms have been swallowed up by suburban sprawl. Nonetheless, covered hoppers still can be found in mixed merchandise trains, delivering grain one carload at a time.

The Manufacturers Railway in St. Louis serves one customer: the Anheuser-Busch brewery. Shipments of grains and other raw products come into the brewery via rail. While it might be fun to think that the tank car being switched is a giant keg of Bud, the reality is the beer leaves by truck.

Above: Sand and salt are two other commodities moved by covered hopper cars. The numbers of carloads of sand have greatly diminished as plastics have replaced glass in consumer packaging. Salt, however, remains a strong commodity on the rails. It is shipped from mines in places like upstate New York and along the Great Salt Lake for use in foods and winter road maintenance.

Left: Hopper cars and gondolas take quite a pounding when they are loaded, and repairs are often needed. Some railroads maintain their own car shops, while others contract the work out. Side-dump hoppers used for carrying copper ore are maintained in the shop of the Copper Basin Railway; when in use, the cars can be loaded and unloaded up to three times a day.

Chapter 3

Flatcars

Flatcars

The most basic of all freight cars—a simple platform mounted on trucks—the flatcar is the foundation for all solid-bottomed freight cars. Add sides, and a flatcar becomes a gondola. Add a roof and it becomes a boxcar.

With no walls to get in the way, flatcars can haul bulky loads that won't fit in gondolas or boxcars. Indeed, the limiting factor for what a flatcar can carry is more likely the clearances along and above the railroad itself. Thus, flatcars are the choice for hauling large, heavy items such as farm machinery.

Over the years, flatcars have seen some adaptations for specialized loads. One of the most basic is the addition of stakes to the sides (either as part of the car or inserted into pockets along the car's frame) to contain loose loads such as raw timber. End walls can be added to flatcars as well to keep loads from shifting forward or backward due to train motion. The lumber industry has also adapted flatcars for specialized loads by adding a center wall down the length of the car. Long strings of these "center-beam" flatcars can be seen coming

from the mills of Canada and the Pacific Northwest (as well as the South), carrying loose long boards or wrapped packages of shorter boards of finished lumber. (One disadvantage of center-beam flats is that a forklift cannot reach both sides of the car for loading or unloading without going around the entire car. Many a forklift operator has tried unloading one side first and then the other, only to have the car tip over halfway through the process due to the weight imbalance!)

The timber industry took the flatcar down to its most basic level for hauling large logs to the mill. To keep the weight of the car to a minimum, flatcars were developed that consisted simply of a center frame with long arms reaching out and up to act as stakes. These bare-bones cars are often called "spider cars" for obvious reasons.

Flatcars were also modified for special use in the 1940s and 1950s as automobiles grew in popularity. Racks were added to the tops of flatcars to provide one or two additional levels for hauling autos. Originally completely open, these colorful trains were rolling advertisements for the newest machines coming out of Detroit. Alas, as times changed, new autos on open racks became targets of vandalism, and autoracks were given side walls and ultimately roofs. Autoracks are often operated as long unit trains looking like giant caterpillars snaking across the landscape.

In addition to carrying bulky loads, another advantage of a flatcar is its ease of loading. Cargo can simply be lifted onto an open flat. When it comes to cargo that can move itself (such as autos and farm machinery), long strings of flatcars can be easily loaded. Called "circus" loading (for one of its earliest and certainly most colorful practitioners), a string of flatcars has plates placed between the ends of adjacent cars, and the first item loaded simply rolls up a ramp onto the last flatcar and keeps rolling until it reaches the first. The circus does indeed still travel by rail, but you're more

apt to see military vehicles traveling on open flats.

For truly heavy, bulky loads such as transformers for generating plants, center-well flatcars were developed. These flats have a depressed center section between the trucks to give more clearance for large loads. Many of these cars have multiple sets of trucks at each end to spread the weight over several axles.

Flatcars were also the earliest cars used for intermodal service, hauling highway trailers long distances, but that's a story unto itself (see Chapter 7).

Thanks to their open design, you're more apt to see unusual loads on a flatcar than on any other type of rolling stock. The aircraft industry has hauled wings and even fuselages on flatcars, and modern windmill farms receive their blades via flats. The rule of thumb is if it won't fit in any other kind of car (and its weatherproof and vandal-proof), put it on a flatcar.

Previous pages: At one time the most basic of all rolling stock, the flatcar has evolved to serve special purposes. Finished lumber rides on flatcars fitted with a center beam and end bulkheads to keep the load from shifting. In addition, rolling stock such as autoracks and gondolas has evolved from the basic design.

Basic flatcars were simply deck-mounted on a frame, useful for carrying bulky loads not affected by the weather. Hooks for tie-downs and pockets for side stakes were provided to secure loads.

The military and the circus use flatcars for the same purpose: transporting vehicles over long distances. In fact, the method of loading a string of flatcars from one end of the string and driving across all the cars to the other end became known as "circus loading." A set of military Hummers ride to their next assignment.

Frames for Ford pickup trucks are stacked on flatcars heading for an assembly plant near Detroit. On the assembly lines, just-in-time inventories require dependable rail transportation, just as Henry Ford believed so many decades ago. In fact, the arches over the train are remnants of an electrified railroad Ford built to serve his growing industry in the 1920s.

Above: Center-beam flatcars feature bulkhead ends and a center divider running the length of the car. The cars are primarily used to haul finished lumber products. While not usually hauled as unit trains, it is not uncommon to see long cuts of center-beams in merchandise trains from the Pacific Northwest.

Right: While it may seem that freight cars are quite stable on their trucks, in fact they are often somewhat precariously balanced. This is most evident with center-beam flatcars. It might be tempting to unload one side of the center-beam first, but more than one forklift operator has caused a flatcar to tip onto its side by uneven unloading.

Quite often, the loads on center-beam cars are wrapped to give some protection from the elements, especially for loads of wallboard or plywood. Long lengths of cut wood, however, are often carried in unwrapped bundles. The cargo is held to the car by metal strapping, which can be quite dangerous if it works loose and flaps from a moving train.

From mills across the rustbelt, steel coils are transported in cars that are part flatcar, part gondola. The coils are secured by bulkheads, and the cars feature a shallow well, which makes them a little more substantial than plain flatcars. Their most identifiable feature, however, is the removable cover to keep rain off the steel.

Above: Locomotives built in the United States and Canada for export are often of a different gauge than North America's standard gauge. Since they can't roll on their own wheels, they are many times shipped from the manufacturer to the port on flatcars. Tarps usually protect the new locomotives from the elements, leaving one to guess just what the departing power looks like.

Left: When it's time to move a railroad maintenance team from one location to another, all the support equipment is placed on flatcars and transported over the tracks. Everything from tampers and ballast cleaners to buses and trucks—and even mobile offices—ride the rails to the next major work project. Major maintenance blitzes can have work crews stationed in one location for weeks at a time.

Above: In 1971, Auto-Train Corporation started carrying passengers between suburban Washington, D.C., and Florida. The passengers' autos rode along on the same train in autoracks. Auto-Train ceased running in 1981, but Amtrak revived the highly successful service in 1983, with 20 or more autoracks heading south and north each day.

Opposite top: The autorack is simply a flatcar with multilevel platforms attached, allowing automobiles to be stacked two or three high. The frame is largely the same as an 80-foot, two-trailer piggyback flatcar. Long strings of autoracks can be loaded at one ramp; the autos can be driven from car to car until the first empty spot is reached. Autoracks are generally found in unit trains—seldom is a single autorack found in a mixed freight.

Opposite bottom: Autoracks started replacing boxcars for shipping new automobiles in the 1950s. A decade later, autos moved exclusively in autoracks. The railroads were reluctant to invest in autoracks, so the Pennsylvania Railroad and Norfolk & Western established Trailer Train Corporation (now TTX) in 1955 to build and lease this specialized equipment. TTX remains one of the largest freight cars leasers.

A gondola is simply a flatcar with four sides. They are useful for transporting heavy loads that are not weather-sensitive, such as steel slabs and scrap metal. It's unusual to find a gondola that isn't dinged and dented, as they seem to be handled more roughly than any other type of car.

Left: Gondolas can be equipped with covers for transporting weather-sensitive cargo. The covers are relatively light and are not completely weather-tight, but they do help keep the gondola's contents dry.

Above: For the enterprising tourist railroad, gondolas can make the ultimate sightseeing car. By cutting an access point into either end (so you can enter the gondola from an adjacent passenger car) and adding a few benches, passengers can enjoy mountain scenery with no obstructions. If it rains, however . . .

Chapter 4

Boxcars

Boxcars

The boxcar has always been the workhorse of the freight car fleet. Offering better cargo protection than flatcars, boxcars have hauled everything from lumber to automobiles. The first boxcars appeared in the 1830s and consisted of a basic frame mounted on two four-wheel trucks. Sliding doors on each side covered an opening of about 6 feet. These early boxcars were about 30 feet in length; by the early 1900s boxcars had grown to about 36 feet in length and could carry about 40 tons.

While boxcars were used for carrying entire loads from point to point, they were also used for "less than carload lot" (LCL) shipments. Every town had a freight house, and when you placed an order from the Sears catalog, for example, your package (no matter how big or small) would arrive at the freight house in a boxcar. Through the end of World War II, railroads served the same function as today's UPS.

As trains grew longer and heavier in the early twentieth century, boxcars were made sturdier with steel under-frames. Wood was still preferred for siding and lining, and during this period the outside-framed wood boxcar came into vogue. As steel became more commonly used in the 1930s, the outside bracing was covered with smooth steel sheathing, although the inside linings generally remained wood.

As automobiles were produced in ever-increasing numbers during this period, some boxcars were manufactured with large sliding double doors for loading Detroit's finest. In the 1940s, warehouses increasingly used forklifts to move palletized cargo and the wide doors developed for automobile loading became standard for all boxcars. In the 1960s, some manufacturers even created all-door boxcars for lumber, but their heavier frames made them less useful for general loading and they soon fell out of favor.

One unique type of boxcar was the stock car, used for hauling livestock. These cars usually had slatted sides for ventilation. During railroading's first century, cattle and other livestock were hauled to big cities for slaughter and preparation. Cattle were driven from the ranch to the railhead and loaded into the stock cars. If the distance to be covered via rail was significant, the cattle were fed, watered, and exercised at line-side pens en route. Stock cars allowed cattle to be raised farther from cities and opened the farmland closer to population centers for vegetable and fruit growing.

The most significant variation of the boxcar is the refrigerator car, commonly called a reefer. Early refrigerator cars, which first appeared in great numbers during the 1860s, were heavily insulated boxcars with roof hatches for loading block ice that was "harvested" from lakes in cold climates during the winter and stored in heavily insulated ice houses where it remained frozen throughout the summer. Electric-powered ice-making plants eventually eliminated the need for harvesting ice. Later, mechanical refrigeration units were mounted to the cars, eliminating the need for re-icing during long trips. Today's refrigerator cars use a cryogen for cooling.

Since refrigerator cars (and the associated ice-producing plants) were used seasonally, railroads were slow to make the investment in the technology. Thus, most refrigerator cars carried the names of the private companies created for the specialized market. Armour was the largest, until antitrust legislation in the early 1900s forced it to divest. Pacific Fruit Express, Fruit Growers Express, and others followed in the private reefer business. Refrigerator cars allowed meat to be processed closer to where cattle were raised, vastly reducing the need for stock cars.

Reefers were the last type of cars made in great quantities from wood, which was a better insulator than steel (the last wooden reefers were made in the 1940s). With the postwar advent of frozen foods, refrigerator cars again became big business. Using ice made with saltwater (which froze at a colder temperature than freshwater), veggies could make the ride from California's lush fields to the Midwest and beyond in frozen comfort. While juice concentrates required temperatures too cold to be kept frozen in reefers, fresh juice could be frozen and shipped from Florida's orange groves to New York; Tropicana purchased its own fleet of cars just for this purpose. Thus, refrigerator cars allowed the largest population centers to receive food from the best farms in the country.

While the typical freight train in the 1950s and 1960s primarily comprised boxcars, a big change was coming. The container revolution of the 1980s and 1990s, while producing trains that looked vastly different, was actually the reinvention of the boxcar.

Previous pages: For most of the history of railroading, the boxcar has been the jack-of-all-trades, carrying just about every commodity that needs protection from theft and the elements. Intermodal operations, where goods are loaded into a container or highway trailer before being placed on the rails, have greatly reduced the boxcar's role.

Right: Early boxcars had steel frames and ends, but the sides were made of wood. The framing for the car was on the outside so the wood walls could serve double-duty as lining on the inside of the car, since exposed framing inside could cause problems by snagging cargo. Wood sides eventually fell out of favor, replaced by steel-sided cars with inside framing and wood lining.

Above: Wood remained a popular choice for boxcar construction into the 1930s, but steel's resistance to weather and abuse soon made it the unanimous choice of material among car builders. By the 1950s very few wooden boxcars were still in service on the major railroads, although some could still be found on narrow gauge lines in Colorado.

The wood lining the inside walls of a typical wood boxcar keep the cargo from snagging on the car's framing. The floor is also wood-covered. Even after the development of steel boxcars, the interior remained largely unchanged. Everything from pallets of paper to sacks of grain can be carried in a boxcar.

Large freight warehouses were used for the transfer of goods from railroads to trucks, especially in the shipment of produce. Long blocks of refrigerated cars were shipped from the fertile fields of California eastward during the spring, arriving at warehouses to be redistributed in trucks over the final miles to market. Most major cities boasted multiple warehouses, as each railroad maintained its own facility.

Above: Refrigerated cars have been used to haul produce, milk, and other perishables, but few were more colorful than the billboard reefers used by brewers. Each car proudly advertised its cargo, whether it was from Milwaukee or the Rocky Mountains. The only problem was the billboard reefers were in the general freight pool, and it was not uncommon for a shipment of Budweiser to wind up in a car with a Miller advertisement. Because of this, advertising on refrigerated cars eventually was eliminated.

Left: The yellow boxcars of Railbox began appearing on U.S. railroads in 1974. Railroads were hampered by a perceived boxcar shortage, caused in part by demurrage rules in effect at the time that required empty cars to be returned to their home road. RailBox, a consortium of several railroads, provided boxcars that didn't need to be returned; once it was empty, it could be loaded again on any railroad.

Right: The refrigerated boxcar opened California's winter produce to a large market, as fresh fruits and vegetables could be shipped to parts of the country where the growing season had ended. Produce could be kept cold and fresh for the 2,000-mile journey to Chicago and St. Louis, or even all the way to New York, some 3,000 miles away. California was truly feeding the nation, thanks to the railroad.

Above: One of the largest privately owned freight car fleets belongs to orange juice producer Tropicana. Each day a long string of the company's refrigerated cars leaves Florida in its own train, bound for the New York metro area. A shorter string of Tropicana reefers is shipped to the Cincinnati area in a regular freight. The solid white "juice train" consist is an impressive sight as it works its way toward New York each morning.

This museum display provides a good perspective on how early refrigerated cars worked. Ice was placed in hatches at the ends of the heavily insulated cars. Trains made stops at icing platforms along the route so the ice could be refreshed. Mechanical refrigeration eventually put an end to the icing operations.

Above: The stock car played a part in the lore of the American West, as cowboys led cattle drives from the grasslands to the railhead. The expanding railroads of the nineteenth century allowed cattle to be raised farther from population centers; it was a short train ride from the Wild West to the famous stockyards of Chicago. In addition to cattle, you could find pigs, poultry, and other livestock in stock cars.

Opposite top: The auto industry has always had a need for boxcars. At one time, finished automobiles were shipped in boxcars, but autoracks have taken over those duties. Today's auto industry relies on components that are manufactured at various sites then combined on the assembly line. Large boxcars handle much of this traffic. The letters DT&I on the side of the boxcar indicate the car is owned by the Detroit, Toledo & Ironton Railroad, a line founded by Henry Ford.

Opposite bottom: Before there was UPS or FedEx, the railroad delivered—and picked up—LCL (less than carload) shipments at every small town along the line. Railroads handled everything from Sears catalog orders to milk from local farmers. As roads and trucks improved, most LCL business moved off the rails. At first, trucks congregated at central points along the railroad to marshal local goods, but eventually nearly all local business turned to the highways.

Chapter 5
Tank Cars

Tank Cars

The most misunderstood freight car on the railroad is the tank car. Vilified by modern media as rolling bombs and potential terrorist targets, many tank cars actually carry benign cargos, while those that carry potentially dangerous materials are almost impossible to breach. There is no safer way to move petroleum products above ground than on a railroad.

Railroads themselves were not eager to embrace tank cars in the mid-1800s because they usually generated revenue in only one direction and returned to their originating points empty. Thus, liquids were usually transported in barrels that could be loaded into boxcars or gondolas that could be used for other commodities on the return trip. Not until the discovery of oil in the United States in 1859 were cars devoted exclusively to hauling liquids deemed necessary.

The earliest true tank cars weren't much more than a pair of open-topped wood vats mounted on a short four-wheel frame. While the railroads were reluctant to invest in tank cars, the oil companies were not, and soon the basic design still in use today was developed: a horizontal tank riding on a pair of four-wheel trucks. Internal baffles kept the liquid from sloshing while in transit, and the tank was slightly tapered toward a central unloading point at the bottom of the car. An extended frame protected the tank in case of a collision, and domes on top allowed for the expansion of the liquid cargo in case of a change in temperature during the trip. Multiple domes indicated the tank car had separate compartments to carry different products simultaneously. Since tank cars could be used for only one type of product (obviously, it would be unwise to load a tank car with crude oil on one trip and vegetable oil on the next), specialized cars became the norm.

The earliest insulated tank cars had wood applied to the outside of the tank. Some cars had piping to heat the inside product (such as molasses) for easier unloading. Depending on the product hauled, special linings were developed—copper for brandy, wooden vats for pickles, and others. Before the era of all-welded tank construction, tank cars often leaked at the seams, so double-riveting was the standard.

In the late 1930s the development of manmade materials such as plastics led to an explosion (figuratively, not literally) of tank car use, as petroleum and chemicals needed to produce these materials took to the rails. Meanwhile, the Southwest oilfields shipped crude to refineries all over the country as the demand for gasoline grew in proportion to America's love affair with the automobile. Tank cars were everywhere. To expedite unloading, piping systems were developed that connected tank cars, allowing multiple cars to be unloaded through one car at one unloading point.

Modern tank cars can be defined by a combination of pressurized or non-pressurized and insulated or non-insulated. Non-pressurized tank cars have the classic dome on top and provision for unloading the car from the bottom. Pressurized cars have no domes and can only be unloaded from the top for safety reasons. Insulated cars have a sheet-metal jacketing over the insulation, which is wrapped around the steel inner tank. Non-insulated cars simply have the steel tank exposed. As tank-construction materials became stronger, the need for a frame was eliminated; most modern tank cars have the tank mounted directly onto the trucks.

Tank cars offer a flexibility that can't be matched by a pipeline. As conditions change and different products are needed at different locations, it is easy to route a tank car with the proper product to the proper destination. Safety is always a concern when hazardous materials are involved, and railroads, unlike trucks on a highway, are isolated from many causes of accidents. Today, myriad hazardous materials from fertilizer to acids travel safely over the rails. The rare accident, however, is often spectacular due to the volumes of product involved.

The next time the media questions the wisdom of running hazardous materials over the nation's rail system, take a moment to reflect on whether you would want all those materials running on the highways where trucks mix with school buses and motorists of questionable skills. The nearly indestructible tank car is the safest way to keep the petroleum and chemical industries humming at optimum output.

Previous pages: The tank car could be considered the most mysterious car on the railroad. Its smooth outer shell hides the secrets within. The car could be carrying something totally innocuous such as talc, or it could contain poisonous chemicals or gases. No wonder no one wants to see a tanker in a derailment.

Above: The earliest tank cars were not much more than a couple of barrels on a flatcar. Murray, Dougal & Company of Milton, Pennsylvania (a predecessor of today's ACF Industries) built the first basic tank car in 1865, and a replica sits in front of the ACF plant today. Note the two-axle truck the car rides on.

Right: By the late 1860s, tank cars had developed into the form that is familiar today. A horizontal metal tank replaced the wooden vats of earlier years. Insulated tank cars appeared in the 1880s, with the earliest covered by wooden slats.

This view provides a good view of the basic layers of the tank. A thin, smooth skin surrounds the outside of the car. A layer of insulation is next, and the actual tank itself is under the insulation. An intact tank car's smooth skin may have a few dents in it, but it's no cause for concern—the interior tank is quite sturdy. This one has a banged-up inside tank and is no longer roadworthy; it is used for locomotive fuel storage.

Most non-pressurized tank cars have the same basic design that lets gravity do all the work. There's a dome at the top for loading contents, and a valve at the bottom for unloading. Most tank cars were built for one commodity (such as oil), which meant they returned to their origin empty and not producing revenue.

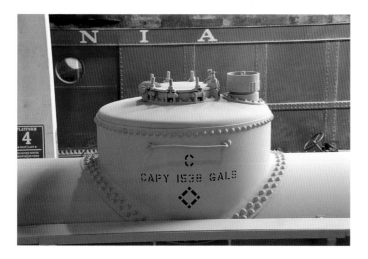

Non-pressurized tank cars feature a dome on top (more than one dome is present if a car has several chambers). The dome allows for filling the car as well as providing room for expansion should the contents become heated. Pressurized tank cars lack a full-sized dome; a much smaller intake protrudes from the top of the car.

North America's railroads own virtually no tank cars, which might come as a surprise, considering entire trains of tank cars can be found on the rails. In reality, most tank cars are owned by private companies such as Union Tank Car. Virtually all modern tank cars use the tank itself as the car's frame.

Chapter 6

Hoppers

Hoppers

Coal and railroads have always gone together. For more than a century, the black diamonds fed the vast majority of hungry steam locomotives. And coal has historically been one of the most stable commodities hauled on the rails.

To haul coal, railroads needed a car that was easy to load and unload, thus the hopper car. With its wide-open top, coal can be loaded into it in a variety of ways (usually by a conveyor as each car proceeds slowly under a loader). Unloading is accomplished by dropping the contents out the bottom of the car, usually into a pit where a conveyor takes the coal to a stockpile or furnace.

Early hopper cars were of wood construction, but the saw-tooth design (whereby coal is unloaded through two or more bottom chutes that look like a saw when the car is viewed in profile) made steel the material of choice, being easier to shape into the unique forms necessary to the design. Originally these cars were constructed with steel sheathing inside of the car's frame. Later, the sheathing was moved to the outside

of the frame, making for a smooth-sided car with less wind resistance and higher interior capacity. Today, however, the sheathing is again generally inside the frame to prevent corrosion of the frame members.

Early hopper cars were short, riding on two or four axles and equipped with drop doors along the bottom. Most coal-loading facilities of the late 1800s were built to load low-profile cars, so when better railroad construction techniques allowed for heavier cars, hopper cars grew in length (looking more like standard gondolas). Eventually, as clearances increased, the cars became taller and shorter, and the saw-tooth bunkers replaced the drop doors. The basic hopper car went largely unchanged until the late twentieth century when smooth-sided aluminum hoppers featuring large drop doors were introduced.

The concept of the unit train—a train that transports just one type of commodity—originated with coal. Early coal mining was done at small mines that could load a few cars a day; railroads gathered loose hopper cars from various sidings and forwarded the cars in general freights to their destination. But the large coal mines that could load an entire train in a day (along with coal consumers such as power plants that could consume entire trainloads in a day) resulted in trains that ran as one unit from origin to destination, bypassing yards and the associated switching en route. The Southern Railway pioneered the unit coal train concept starting in 1960. Today, the unit train concept has spread to everything from automobiles to piggyback service.

It should be noted that sometimes things aren't what they appear to be. You might think you're watching a coal train made up entirely of hopper cars, but you could be wrong. Modern unloading techniques have led to the rotary dump car, which allow the contents to leave the same way they got in: out the top. With specially designed couplers, these cars can stay attached to each other and still be completely inverted for unloading, eliminating the need for doors on the bottoms of the cars. That unit coal train is not made up of hopper cars—it's made up of large gondolas!

Watching all the coal and intermodal trains rolling through all corners of North America, you might think the hopper car, piggyback flats, or container cars are the most common types of rolling stock. Surprisingly, however, the covered hopper car is the most common type of car. The major difference between a hopper car and a covered hopper is the latter's covered top with hatches for loading.

Grain was the first commodity hauled in covered hoppers, starting around 1830. But since their use was restricted to the harvest season, railroads were slow to embrace them. Less seasonal commodities, such as zinc, were hauled in covered hoppers in the very early 1900s, but only in limited quantities. By the 1920s, though, phosphate rock was being carried in covered hoppers as well.

By the 1940s grain had taken to the rails again. Being relatively light, more grain could be placed on a set of trucks and the size of covered hoppers grew. In 1953 an unloading system was created that used air to help evacuate the contents of covered hoppers, which began carrying denser commodities such as flour. While early covered hoppers were rectangular with ribbed sides, today you'll find clay, starch, cement, sand, grain, and many other commodities inside smooth cylindrical cars.

Previous pages: The Bone Valley near Tampa, Florida, is a large producer of phosphate, which keeps the railroads busy. Long strings of covered hopper cars are loaded at several mines in the valley and taken north by CSX. Covered hopper cars are also used for grains, plastic pellets, and other bulk commodities. Through trains often keep the same power, even when changing railroads. This BNSF locomotive has found its way onto CSX tracks.

Standard hopper cars are used for hauling cargo that can be loaded and unloaded in bulk, and which is not affected by weather. Primary among these commodities is coal, which has been one of the most reliable revenue sources for railroads. Until the late twentieth century, hopper cars could be found scattered throughout any general merchandise freight train, but in the twenty-first century they are far more common in unit trains. Hoppers are loaded from the top, with hatches (in this instance two) for unloading.

Left: A long string of hopper cars stands ready to receive taconite pellets from a Great Lakes ship. In most instances, unit hopper trains operate from a single loading point—a mine or a transloading facility—to a single destination. Final consumers can include power plants for coal shipments or processing plants for ores.

Above: The unit train wasn't invented in the 1980s, although that's when the concept was fully developed. Coal haulers used the unit train concept beginning in the earliest parts of the twentieth century to haul "black diamonds" from the mine to the processing plant. The East Broad Top, located in central Pennsylvania, ran trains north to a connection with the Pennsylvania Railroad, where the coal was sorted and transferred. The lone boxcar is for LCL freight.

Right: Coal heads from the mine to a power plant in Arizona on the electrified Black Mesa & Lake Powell. Modern hopper cars are often made of aluminum, which is lightweight yet strong enough for heavier loads. The electric locomotives are powered by the product they're hauling, albeit indirectly—the power to the overhead wires comes from a coal-fired generating plant.

Above: If you see a long unit coal train coming from the west, odds are it originated in the Powder River Basin in Wyoming and Montana. Coal is located near the surface in this region, allowing inexpensive mining. The coal is unloaded from these hoppers the same way it went in: from the top. The light paint at the front of hoppers indicates a rotary coupler is located on that end of the car, allowing for the entire car to be turned upside down and dumped without uncoupling it from adjacent cars.

Copper ore mined in southeastern Arizona is carried by train from the mine to the smelter. The Copper Basin Railway makes several roundtrips a day to keep the smelter going. Unlike traditional hopper cars, these cars unload from the side instead of the bottom; the side panel swings out, allowing the contents to empty. The faster the cars unload, the sooner the train can make another trip.

Is it a tank car or a hopper car? It has top hatches and no dome, so it must be a covered hopper car. But it has no bottom hatches, so maybe it's a tank car. Designed to carry powdered cement, this car shows that classifying freight cars into broad categories is not an exact science. Often, the commodity dictates the development of a special hybrid car.

Above: The short wheelbase and high sides indicate this hopper car is used for carrying ballast. Railroads use ballast to give the right-of-way stability and to promote good drainage. Since ballast is usually a lightweight material such as limestone, more volume can be carried in a single car. The ballast is spread onto the right-of-way directly through the car's bottom hatches as the train proceeds at a walking pace. Usually a crewman will walk along the train to open hatches as each car is emptied.

Left: Locomotives are equipped with devices that spread sand directly in front of their wheels to provide traction on wet rails. This sand is brought to the engine terminal in covered hoppers that are often dedicated just for this service. Penn Central, like other railroads, put a large "S" on the side of hoppers that were in company sand service.

Above: Long trains of covered hopper cars carry wheat and flour from the Midwest. While much of the region's production moves on water (as evidenced by the barges on the Mississippi River in St. Paul, Minnesota), railroads still handle a substantial portion; much wheat and flour travels by both modes, transported by rail from the grain elevators to transloading points.

Right: Some bulk-loaded commodities need to be kept out of the weather, hence the covered hopper car. These cars have several roof hatches and unload from the bottom. Grain and some mined products are the primary commodities found in covered hopper cars.

Covered hoppers come in two basic designs: rectangular with outside bracing and cylindrical. The vast majority of covered hoppers in Canada are cylindrical, moving wheat from the prairie provinces of Saskatchewan and Alberta across the Rocky Mountains to tidewater at Vancouver, British Columbia. Many of Canada's covered hoppers are owned by the provinces they serve.

Chapter 7

Intermodal

Intermodal

I f one were to stand by any major North American transcontinental main line in the 1970s and then stand by that same line today, what would be different? Certainly the locomotives are larger, but the trains themselves are pretty much the same. There are mixed-commodity trains, unit trains, and even trailers on flatcars. But one kind of train today didn't exist in the 1970s: the train carrying cargo containers stacked two high on well cars. These "double-stack" trains can reach lengths of 2 or 3 miles.

The development of the stack train can be traced to two factors. First is North America's insatiable appetite for Asian-made goods, most of which arrive on huge cargo vessels. The second factor goes back more than a century to the building of the Panama Canal. The canal's builders never envisioned the size of today's container ships, thus the canal is too narrow. With all these goods entering the continent on the Pacific Coast, but most of the population living near the Atlantic, there are two options: ship the goods around South America or send them east across land. Shipping containers are the perfect size to be

placed on railcars, and by creating well cars with deep bottoms that almost touch the rails, two containers can be stacked and still accommodate clearances.

The stack train is getting ahead of the intermodal story, however. The more traditional approach to intermodal railroading is placing highway trailers on flatcars. The first examples of this occurred in the 1800s on the Long Island Rail Road (granted, the trailers were pulled by horses and the highway system wasn't much back then). The first continuous haulage of highway trailers on flatcars was instituted by the Chicago Great Western in the 1930s. Nonetheless, there were those in the highway industry that refused to cooperate with the railroads, and vice versa, so the intermodal movement got off to a slow start. Trailers on flatcars (TOFC) finally took off in the 1950s when the Interstate Commerce Commission removed many of the regulatory barriers that separated highway, marine, and rail shipping modes.

The first intermodal freight cars were simply flatcars with the highway trailers secured using the trailer's "fifth wheel" hub.

Two trailers of the 1950s could fit on one flatcar. As trailers grew in size, so did the flatcars, eventually reaching 89 feet in length. For the most part, both the flatcars and the highway trailers were provided by private companies at a time when most railroad cars were owned by the railroads. Eventually, special-use cars were developed for intermodal use, including spine cars, which are not much more than a frame riding on four wheels yet capable of holding a trailer.

While trailer-loading was initially cumbersome at best—trailers were loaded using the "circus" method, whereby one trailer was pushed to the far end of a cut of flatcars, then a tractor clattered over the entire cut to get a second trailer and so forth—methods were developed to physically lift trailers onto railcars. Terminals were built specifically for intermodal as increased loading speeds became essential for the railroads to compete with over-the-road trucking.

Perhaps the ultimate in self-contained intermodal was developed by the Chesapeake & Ohio after World War II. The C&O integrated a freight car frame into a standard highway trailer to create the RoadRailer—a trailer with both rubber tires and flanged wheels. The C&O was quite ahead of its time, and the concept didn't really take off until the 1980s. Too light to be integrated into regular freight trains, RoadRailers could be coupled to the back of passenger trains (as C&O did) or run in solid sets. RoadRailers have become somewhat common in the northeastern United States, particularly on Norfolk Southern's Triple Crown service. RoadRailers are at their best where the over-the-road haul from the terminal is fairly short, as the railcar frame is quite heavy and uneconomical for lengthy runs behind a highway tractor. In the 1990s, Amtrak experimented with RoadRailers as a way to generate revenue for its passenger trains.

So is the intermodal car the modern flatcar? At first glance one might think so, but in actuality it is the modern boxcar. At one time boxcars were used to deliver less-than-carload (LCL) shipments to every small hamlet on the railroad's system. Today that same function is carried out by the highway trailer or container. The only difference is that the beginning and end of the journey is often not along the railroad.

Previous pages: Among the lightest railcars are those used in intermodal service, both piggyback and containers. And because they are light, they can be combined into some of the longest trains you'll see. A piggyback train wraps itself around Tehachapi Loop in Southern California heading out of the Los Angeles Basin.

Right: In the early days of intermodal railroading (just after World War II) highway trailers were simply placed on flatcars for transport. Ultimately, TrailerTrain developed long, light flatcars that could hold two standard highway trailers. In modern railroading, the flatcar has been replaced by lightweight articulated frames that have a well for the trailer's tires and a fifth-wheel hitch to hold the front of the trailer.

Above: Among the advantages rail has over highway is that a trailer can be on the move for days without the need for driver rest. Busy intermodal terminals are 24-hour-a-day operations, although trailers usually are marshaled throughout the day for an evening rail departure. Most intermodal trains arrive at their destination terminal before daybreak so the trailers can be delivered during normal working hours.

This view of a modern intermodal car shows the trailer wheel platforms and fifth-wheel hitch. Riding the cars are empty highway frames used for transporting containers over the road. The empty cars and empty frames indicate that this train isn't making a whole lot of money for anybody.

Most railroads, especially in the East, had to make major clearance improvements to handle the explosion of container traffic entering North America from Asia. Stacking containers two high made for a very efficient method of moving cargo, but all across the country tunnel roofs had to be raised (or floors dropped), underpasses had to be elevated, and overhead structures had to be removed to allow a clearance of 20 feet 2 inches.

Left: A full set of two-axle trucks is often unnecessary to accommodate the weight of an intermodal car and container. What appear to be three cars directly behind the locomotive is actually a three-unit articulated car (considered one car by the railroads). The middle unit shares a four-axle truck with both the first and third unit, saving the weight of one complete truck set.

Above: Containers are moved in well cars, with the floor of the car barely above the railhead. A container fits inside the well, and fittings allow containers to be firmly stacked two high on the railroad (and up to eight high on ships and in terminals). The low-slung cars provide lowered centers of gravity and keep the overall height to just over 20 feet.

Above: The RoadRailer concept is quite logical: take the advantages of moving highway trailers by both rail and road, but eliminate the railcar. The resulting car can be moved in unit trains of like cars, or even at the end of passenger trains. The big advantages include rail diesel fuel savings and time savings at the terminal when transferring the trailer from rail to road. The big disadvantage is the extra weight the trailers have on the roads, as all the railroad apparatus stays on the unit. For short hauls from terminal to final destination, however, the RoadRailer concept is very economical.

Right: RoadRailers have many advantages over conventional piggyback service. With no piggyback car required, it takes half the fuel to move the same number of trailers. And since the trailers aren't lifted by cranes, there is less shifting of the trailer's contents. RoadRailer trailers also have more capacity than a standard cargo container, and are more rugged.

While early RoadRailers had railroad wheels attached directly to the trailer, the Triple Crown fleet (some 7,000 trailers strong) rides on a two-axle bogie placed between each trailer. The bogies provide a solid connection with no slack between the trailers, eliminating damage from rough starting and stopping. And with only 12 inches between the trailers, theft from a RoadRailer trailer is virtually impossible.

Amtrak experimented with carrying express in the 1990s, in what was perhaps a misguided effort to increase revenues. Amtrak used RoadRailer trailers attached to the rear of regular passenger trains. Alas, the delays in adding and taking off the express cars resulted in lackluster timekeeping for the passengers, and express service was discontinued.

Left: Intermodal trains bypass freight yards and are instead assembled in dedicated facilities. These intermodal yards are located near major metropolitan centers with good access to interstate highways to expedite the final delivery of containers and trailers. Well cars are loaded using mobile overhead gantries.

Above: There is nothing more discouraging to a railroad's accountant than the "bare table" train, which consists of empty piggyback flats or container well cars. These trains generate no revenue, as there is no freight on board.

Chapter 8
Maintenance-of-Way Equipment

Maintenance-of-Way Equipment

Walk around any freight yard and you'll see nonrevenue cars—cars that are necessary to railroad operations but generate no revenue. Most of these cars are used for the upkeep of the railroad's physical plant.

Some nonrevenue cars might not be obvious. What appear to be conventional covered hopper cars sitting near the locomotive-servicing area are actually cars used for storing sand (locomotives have rail sanders to give them extra traction on wet rails). What appear to be ore cars could very well be ballast cars, spreading rock along the right-of-way. Gondolas can be used for everything from junk storage to hauling scrap. And flatcars see all kinds of service, including carrying rail-mounted maintenance vehicles such as ballast cleaners.

But special-purpose nonrevenue cars are found around the yard as well. The most eye-catching are snowplows, which come in

two main varieties. The most basic simply have a wedge plow mounted on the front of a modified gondola. The gondola is loaded with concrete or other heavy material for weight. Wedge plows are almost exclusively non-powered and are pushed by a locomotive.

The heavy hitter in the snow battle is the rotary plow. Introduced in 1883, rotaries have a set of fan-like blades mounted in the front and can toss snow 30 yards or more. California's Donner Pass has frequently seen rotary plows clear the right-of-way of the wet and heavy Sierra snows that crews call "concrete." A wedge plow would simply not be able to penetrate the larger drifts. Rotary plows were steam-driven until the 1980s, but as their numbers have dwindled the survivors have been converted to diesel. The power inside a rotary simply powers the blades; all propulsion comes from locomotives.

The close cousin to the wedge plow is the flanger. With adjustable blades that can be extended well outside the width of the right-of-way, the flanger keeps ballast trimmed and the rails clear of debris. Flangers can also be used for snow removal.

Every now and then you might see a diminutive four-wheel box rolling along behind a freight. This is a scale-test car. For bulk commodities such as coal and ores, railroads bill a shipper by the ton, so the weight of the shipment needs to be determined. Scales are built at various points on the system, and by weighing the car and its contents and subtracting the car's weight the billable weight can be determined. These scales needed to be calibrated, so a scale-test car, which weighs a known amount, is dispatched to the scale. These cars need to be calibrated themselves, which is done at a major terminal.

Given the weights and speeds of modern freight trains, wear and tear to the track needs to be addressed constantly. One of the most spectacular maintenance exercises is rail-grinding. Corrugation of the railhead is a natural occurrence as steel wheels hammer steel rails, and the grinder smoothes the surface. It's a high-friction operation, and sparks will fly. To mitigate the danger of line-side fires, a car equipped with a fire hose and a few tank cars are the last few cars on the train.

A variety of cranes can also be found in the railroad environment. "Big hooks" once helped in wreck cleanups, using steam power to do the lifting. They were ferried to wreck sites within work trains. In modern railroading, there are companies that specialize in wreck cleanups, so most railroads no longer maintain their own large cranes. Today's large cranes get close to wreck sites via the highway system, dispatched from the cleanup company's terminal. Once they get as close to the site as they can via road, the cranes then take to the rails if necessary to reach the derailment.

Finally, all the maintenance work requires people. Major maintenance projects can require a work crew to be onsite for weeks at a time. Special camp cars can be spotted near a work site, providing lodging and dining facilities for extended stays. At one time, these camp cars resembled modified boxcars, with windows in the sides and end doors. The modern camp car is more likely to be a prefabricated office placed on a normal flatcar.

They don't make money, but they keep the railroad moving. If the world of railroading is a big stage, then maintenance cars are the stagehands.

Previous pages: A heavy crane and a rotary snowplow in the Nevada Northern's shop in Ely await their next call to duty. Any railroad that owns a heavy crane or a snowplow will be happy to have both pieces of equipment sit unused—when either is called out, it's usually bad news. Derailments and major snowstorms are just two of many maintenance headaches facing the railroads.

Where there's a railroad, there's going to be the occasional derailment and the even rarer wreck. Until the late twentieth century, railroads owned heavy cranes that could lift freight and passenger cars, and even locomotives. These cranes traveled in work trains to the derailment site. Often a neighboring railroad's crane would be borrowed so cleanup work could take place at both ends of a wreck.

Above: Steam-powered heavy cranes remained in service into the 1960s. Then, as with locomotives, diesel power became the norm. Most railroads have stopped maintaining their own cranes, relying instead on outside contractors such as Hulcher or R. J. Corman for derailment cleanups. Alas, contractors use cranes that operate over the highways to a wreck site, and few rail-mounted heavy cranes remain in service.

Left: Most rail-mounted cranes in modern railroading are used for maintenance. The cranes are designed to lift rail and ties, but are not equipped to lift other rail equipment. Rail-mounted cranes usually are accompanied by a flatcar that serves as an idler car for the boom.

Above: To house maintenance workers in remote areas, railroads employ camp cars. These motels on wheels are parked on sidings, and workers return to them each night, saving a long trip back to civilization. Some railroads operate weekly employee-only passenger trains to take workers from camp cars back to their home terminal on weekends. Modern camp cars are prefabricated cabins placed on flatcars.

Right: The most common type of snowplow is the wedge plow, which simply pushes the snow off to either side of the right-of-way. These plows were pushed by a locomotive and usually were not added to the front of a freight train—the locomotive and plow would go out alone to clear the tracks. The Long Island Rail Road had one of the more creatively painted wedge plows.

Continuous welded rail—also called "ribbon rail"—is carried on flatcars equipped with special racks to accommodate 9 to 12 lengths of rail. As the rail can be nearly a quarter-mile long, a single train may only have a dozen rails on it. The flatcars often appear in work trains with automatic track-laying machinery.

Above: To accurately weigh the cargo in a car (such as the amount of coal in a hopper car), railroads have scales located at various locations along their routes. To ensure accuracy, scale-test cars that have been precisely weighed at a major shop are dispatched to calibrate the remote scales. This homebuilt scale-test car was made from the pilot wheels of a steam locomotive and was used to calibrate scales weighing cars carrying copper ore.

Opposite top: The best efficiency of steel wheel on steel rail occurs when the rail surface is smooth, so railroads periodically grind the rails of main-line trackage (usually through a contractor). The rail grinder polishes the surface in a shower of sparks and a haze of smoke. Water cars and a hose car trail the train to put out any line-side fires.

Opposite bottom: The flanger is the jack-of-all-trades in railroad maintenance. With a large front plow and extendable side wings, it is used for clearing debris from tracks, and for clearing snow in regions where snowfall amounts don't warrant the use of a plow. Flangers often accompany work trains that spread ballast.

Chapter 9

Baggage Cars and RPOs

Baggage Cars and RPOs

A typical long-distance passenger train once comprised coaches, dining cars, sleeping cars, and perhaps an observation car. Usually, these trains also had a car without a single ticketed passenger aboard. That car was the workhorse of the fleet: the baggage car.

Baggage cars fall into the broader category of "head-end cars," so called because of their position in the train, normally directly behind the locomotives.

Long-distance travel once meant a lot of luggage, and from the earliest days of rail travel coaches were not exactly roomy. Aisles were narrow and ceiling height was restricted. Even parlor and sleeping cars had tight spaces. Thus it was in the best interest of operations and passenger comfort to keep luggage out of the way. On the railroad, checked bags went into (and still go into) the baggage car. You had to be very mindful about what you put in your carry-on bag, because on a train you and your checked baggage could be separated for days, not just hours.

While early baggage cars were undoubtedly boxcars pressed into passenger service, soon specialized cars were designed. Baggage cars usually had one or more large cargo doors on each side for quick loading of bulky trunks. Racks and tie-down loops were added to secure cargo. As passenger train speeds increased, the baggage cars were placed on passenger-car trucks.

Not all passenger trains required a full baggage car. Trains on less-traveled routes or branch lines often needed only a portion of a car devoted to baggage. Thus, the combination car, or "combine," came into use. Usually, combines had a baggage area at the front third of the car, with the rest of the car devoted to traditional coach seating. Mixed trains (passenger and freight cars in the same train) that carried few passengers often used a lone combine to handle passenger traffic.

While the head end of a passenger train often had baggage cars, there were also other cars located near the locomotives. A close relative of the baggage car is the express car, used to carry expedited commercial loads. Express cars were boxcars mounted on trucks that could handle passenger train speeds. Railway Express Agency was the dominate company in this business during much of the first half of the twentieth century. Express traffic could consist of anything from medicines to newspapers. After most express traffic moved to planes and trucks in the late twentieth century, Amtrak experimented with operating express cars but found that the additional logistics of mixing express with passenger operations put them at a disadvantage against other modes of transportation. Today, FedEx and UPS have taken the place of railway express, but one might be surprised to learn that today's financial giants Wells Fargo and American Express actually have roots in the business.

Perhaps the most glamorous of the head-end cars was the Railway Post Office, or RPO. Before the rail network was developed, mail was handled on foot or horseback. Railroads cut days (and in some cases weeks) off mail delivery times. Special RPO cars were built to handle mail. Looking much like a baggage car from the outside, the interior was quite different. Slots and sack holders allowed for sorting of mail while the train was en route. In towns where passenger trains did not stop, a hook from the RPO could snag a sack of mail from special stanchions; simultaneously, a postal employee would toss a sack containing the town's incoming mail off the train. RPO service lasted into the 1970s before vanishing. On some remote routes in Canada, mail is still carried in sacks on passenger trains, but it is sorted beforehand.

Mail and express played a pivotal role in passenger train history. As more and more travelers went by car or airplane in the 1950s and train riders became fewer, mail and express business kept many passenger trains running, subsidizing the mounting losses. Few trains were left by 1971, when Amtrak was formed that year to take over the money-losing passenger trains from the railroads. With rail travel making a comeback in the twenty-first century, we have express business and those non-passenger-carrying head-end cars to thank for getting the passenger train through its leanest times.

Previous pages: As passengers board at a major station, few pause to notice all the activity at the head end of the train. Baggage and packages are loaded and unloaded quickly, perishables are brought aboard, and express cars see a rapid exchange of less-than-carload (LCL) traffic.

Right: The baggage car is simply a small warehouse on wheels, carrying large pieces of luggage that would be checked at a passenger's departing depot. In today's world, travelers are accustomed to checking bags at airports, and the railroads have provided the same service on most long-distance trains. The baggage car was usually located near the locomotives in a passenger consist.

Above: Amtrak and VIA Rail Canada still offer checked baggage services on long-distance trains. VIA's *Canadian,* which travels between Toronto and Vancouver, is an all-stainless-steel train with equipment built by the Budd Company. Bags are off-loaded from the baggage car into carts, which carry them into the depot's baggage room to be claimed by their owners. It is very similar to what the airlines offer, only the entire process is far more visible to passengers.

The close cousin of the baggage car is the express car. Rather than carrying checked bags, the express car carries time-sensitive shipments, often point-to-point, at passenger train speeds (which, in pre-airline days, was the fastest service available). Express cars were located at the front of passenger trains. If a train carried several express cars, it was said the train had a lot of "head-end traffic." Some express cars looked like typical baggage cars, while some more closely resembled boxcars (albeit on high-speed trucks).

Above: The combination car, or "combine," was used on lines where patronage was light and, thus, a full baggage car wasn't needed to handle the volume of checked bags. While combines could be of various makeups, the most common was the baggage/coach combine, where the front third of the car was devoted to bag-handling, while standard passenger seating occupied the rear two-thirds.

Opposite top: As the automobile became more common and passenger counts diminished on branch lines, many railroads combined their passenger and freight traffic into one train. While this wasn't the fastest way for passengers to get from point to point, these "mixed" trains kept rail passenger service alive on light-density lines for a few extra years. Given the lack of patronage on these branches, a lone combine at the end of the freight often was sufficient to handle all the passengers and their bags. On some very lightly used lines, passengers were simply put in the freight's caboose.

Opposite bottom: While looking like a standard baggage car, this century-old product of American Car & Foundry is actually a combination baggage/Railway Post Office car. The baggage portion occupies most of the space, while the post office is in the forward 15 feet, served by the small door at the front of the car. Interestingly, to prevent mail robberies, there is no door inside the car between the two sections; a solid wall separates the baggage and post office sections. The only way into the post office is through the side doors.

Above: Another baggage car cousin is the Railway Post Office, or "RPO." In pre-highway days, the railroads were the most efficient means to move the U.S. Mail. Special cars were employed for this service, staffed by government employees. Like baggage cars, RPOs were carried at the front of passenger trains. Most RPOs were painted the same color as the railroad's passenger equipment.

Right: For many small towns, this was the mailbox: a simple slot in the side of an RPO. If the letter was going to one of the towns the RPO served later that day, it would likely be sorted en route and dropped the same day. Otherwise, it would be combined with other mail going to an off-line destination and bagged for further sorting and later delivery.

An RPO carried all the necessities for handling mail. Sorting tables and small bins were provided to sort letters en route. Bags were used to pick up and drop off mail at various towns. On passenger trains that didn't stop at small towns, the bags were thrown from the moving train onto the station platform, and a hook was used to snatch mailbags from trackside stanchions "on the fly."

Chapter 10
Coaches

Coaches

Shortly after the railroads came into being in the 1820s and it became apparent that passengers could be carried on rails, railroads began developing cars that were essentially stagecoaches and even buggies on railroad wheels. All early passenger cars rode on just four wheels, making for a bumpy ride on the crude track of the day.

Passenger cars soon grew in length, however, and with the growth came a much-improved ride from a pair of four-wheel trucks. Springing was improved and the added weight made for a more stable ride. Interior seating was arranged to provide more room and comfort for passengers. By 1860 the passenger car had achieved the classic look that remains to this day, although construction materials have changed through the decades.

Early cars had little or no heat. Coal-fired stoves were the first heating appliances used in passenger coaches, beginning in the 1830s. The heat was unevenly distributed and the flames generated by the stoves were a hazard in wooden cars. By the beginning of the twentieth century, steam heat was common in coaches, with steam drawn directly from the locomotive. This practice remained in use well into the diesel years of railroading. In fact, many railroads purchased diesel locomotives with steam generators for passenger service.

Other than iron framing, early passenger cars were constructed entirely of wood. Truss rods kept the cars from sagging and the whole thing was held together with nails, screws, and glue. As car lengths grew to 80 feet, steel construction became more economical and in wrecks was less susceptible to splintering and fire. What really sold the railroads on all-steel cars, though, was the development of the steel subway car in New York City in 1903. The Pennsylvania Railroad decided to use steel for many of the same reasons the subway did—primarily because wooden cars were not a very good idea in tunnels, and the Pennsy had long tunnels leading into Manhattan's Penn Station. It would be the 1920s, however, before steel cars outnumbered wooden cars on the railroads, and some wooden cars could be found in use into the 1950s.

The first quarter of the twentieth century was known as the "heavyweight era" on the railroads, as most passenger cars were, well, heavy. The cars were long (85 feet in some instances), rode on a pair of six-wheel trucks, and were increasingly built from steel. All this changed in the 1930s when streamlining became the rage. Art deco designs, fueled by the public's infatuation with airplanes, were applied to railcars and train stations. The Budd Company produced the stainless-steel *Zephyr* trainsets for the Chicago, Burlington & Quincy, and the *Pioneer Zephyr's* transcontinental run generated so much publicity that there was more demand than the new trains could accommodate. Part of the problem was that early streamliners were semi-permanently coupled sets: a sleek, shovel-nosed locomotive, a handful of cars tagging along, and a round-end observation car. These sets could not be easily added to, and if any unit of the set needed repair the entire set was sidelined. The Milwaukee Road's *Hiawathas* were the first non-coupled streamline sets. Soon, large similar fleets were entering service in the East.

Experiments to produce even lighter cars began with the General Motors–produced Train of Tomorrow in 1947. These trains featured cars with low centers of gravity for added speed in curves and extremely light weights for better fuel economy. Airlines and highways were already making inroads into the railroads' passenger business, and cost-cutting was necessary. The New York Central's Xplorer used about a quarter of the fuel of a conventional passenger train on the Cleveland–Cincinnati run. However, all of these experimental lightweight trains had a major fault: they didn't ride well. Most were semi-permanently coupled, with adjacent cars sharing a single two-wheel truck at each end, and their light weight worked against them on rough track.

Most railroads exited the long-distance passenger train business in 1971 when Amtrak was formed to take over money-losing operations. Amtrak's first new coaches were tubular cars (much like airliner fuselage) based on the Metroliner developed by the Pennsylvania in 1965. These Amfleet cars still comprise the backbone of the passenger car fleet in the East. For many of Amtrak's trains outside the Northeast (where vertical clearances are greater), the double-deck Superliner car has become standard. As Amtrak continues to draw passengers, it won't be long before another generation of passenger car is developed.

Previous pages: Outside the busy station in San Jose a commuter train with modern bi-level cars awaits the rush hour. Highway-happy California has embraced the passenger train with modern commuter lines and state-sponsored Amtrak service reaching out of the Bay Area and Los Angeles. The San Jose–to–San Francisco corridor has seen some of the most modern trainsets in North America placed into service.

The earliest coaches were not much more than horse carriages mounted on large flanged wheels. The DeWitt Clinton operated along the Mohawk River in New York State starting in 1831. Early steam locomotives emitted a lot of hot debris, so the ride on the top seats of the coaches must have been an interesting experience.

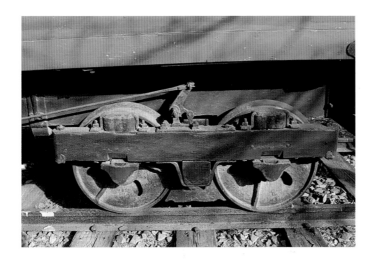

Left: Early coaches rode on wood-framed trucks and used a manual braking system controlled by a lever in each car. By the late nineteenth century, all-metal trucks had replaced wooden trucks, and by the early twentieth century, cast-steel trucks were common. The invention of the airbrake in 1869 allowed all cars in a train to be braked from the locomotive.

Above: Passenger cars quickly evolved into the basic design that is still used today. The cars were extended and placed on a pair of two-axle trucks. Clerestory windows along the roof allowed for ventilation and light. Early coaches had open vestibules at both ends, making passing between cars an open-air experience.

Right: The interior design of a passenger coach has remained unchanged for more than a century. A center aisle with two seats on both sides is the standard. Some commuter coaches have 3-2 seating (three seats on one side, two on the other), and the number of rows of seats depends on the car's use; long-distance coaches had fewer rows, and thus more legroom.

Above: Harriman cars (named after railroad baron E. H. Harriman) were some of the first all-steel cars, with the earliest appearing in 1906. The cars featured enclosed vestibules. Harriman controlled many railroads and believed in standardization, so these cars rapidly appeared all across the country. Many lasted in regular service into the 1960s.

The Pennsylvania Railroad built the first P70 coach in 1907, and it became one of the most famous coach designs in history. The cars featured enclosed vestibules and a wider-than-normal clerestory. Pennsy built the first car at its shop in Altoona, Pennsylvania, but subsequent cars were built by Bethlehem Steel and Pressed Steel Car Company.

The Southern Railway's coaches of the 1920s and 1930s were typical heavyweights of the era. Southern's coaches were made of steel and built by Pullman. Heavyweight coaches rode on a pair of three-axle trucks, which allowed for a smoother ride. The car's weight also contributed to the quality of the ride—the heavier the car, the less it bounced.

Left: The streamlined era ushered in lighter trains, with builders like the Budd Company producing passenger cars. Canadian Pacific's premier train, the *Canadian,* was an all-Budd train with stainless-steel cars. Other railroads, including the Santa Fe and the Burlington, also featured trainsets of stainless cars. VIA Rail still operates the Canadian Pacific Budd-built cars on today's version of the *Canadian.*

Above: In 1944, Cyrus Osborne, working for locomotive manufacturer Electro-Motive Division (General Motors), was riding in the cab of a streamlined locomotive through the Rocky Mountains. He marveled at the engineer's view out the front windows. Osborne applied that view to a passenger car and the first dome car was invented. First used by the Burlington, the idea soon spread to many railroads operating in the West.

Right: In 1934, the Union Pacific introduced the *City of Salina,* the railroad's first streamlined train. Fully air conditioned and featuring impeccable service, the smooth-sided streamliners set a new standard for rail travel. Union Pacific would eventually add nine more streamlined sets to the fleet. Some of those streamlined cars are retained into the twenty-first century for use on UP's business train.

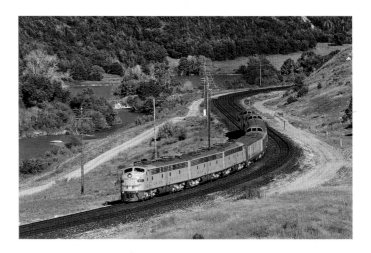

Above: One of the most famous streamliners was the *California Zephyr,* which operated with Budd-built stainless-steel cars. The *Zephyr* was jointly operated by the Burlington, the Rio Grande, and the Western Pacific between Chicago and Oakland. When Amtrak was formed in 1971, the Rio Grande opted out of the agreement and the *Zephyr* became the last classic streamliner in the United States, operating until 1983.

The last great streamliner in North America is VIA Rail's *Canadian,* operating between Toronto and Vancouver. Summertime consists sometimes exceed 25 cars, and the entire train is still made up of 1950s-vintage Budd-built stainless-steel cars. With domes, diners, coaches, and a round-end dome-observation car, it is truly the last of the classic trains.

When Amtrak was created in 1971 to relieve U.S. railroads of money-losing passenger trains, it inherited a ragged fleet of second-hand coaches. In 1975, Amtrak ordered its first new coaches: 492 Amfleet cars from the Budd Company. Based on the Metroliner design of 1979, the cars were placed in service throughout Amtrak's system.

Above: Starting in 1981, Amtrak ordered an additional set of 150 Amfleet cars. Both orders came in a variety of configurations, including short-haul and long-haul coaches (long-haul coaches have more legroom), cafés, dinettes, club cars, and lounges. Externally, the cars all looked alike, with the exception of the window configuration near the middle on the café cars.

Left: Delivery of Superliner equipment, as well as new cars from Bombardier for West Coast operations, allowed Amtrak to consign its Amfleet cars to East Coast operations. Designed for high-speed and the clearances of the tunnels into New York City, the cars remain the workhorses of Amtrak's Northeast Corridor operations, even though the newest Amfleet cars are more than a quarter-century old.

Above: When Amtrak modernized its fleet of long-distance coaches in the late 1970s, it turned to Pullman-Standard to build bi-level "Superliners" in various configurations. Featuring large windows for viewing the countryside, most passenger seating is located on the car's second level. The cars' design was based on the Santa Fe's high-level cars built by Budd in the 1950s.

Right: When Amtrak purchased its first Superliners, it acquired coaches, sleepers, and dining cars. The coaches were delivered first and were used on short-haul trains throughout 1979. Once the other cars arrived on the property, the coaches were transferred to their intended long-distance service. Most Superliner coaches have lower-level seating as well as high-level seating, but some are actually combines, with baggage storage on the lower level.

Amtrak's initial Superliner order with Pullman-Standard included 102 coaches with seating on both levels, and 48 combines with baggage rooms on the lower level. By the time the second Superliner order was placed in the early 1990s, Pullman's designs had been purchased by Bombardier; another 38 coaches were added to the roster at this time. Prior to the later order, the Superliners were used almost exclusively on western routes. Once the second order was delivered, most Amtrak routes not serving the close clearances of New York City were Superliner-equipped.

In the twentieth century there were many attempts to increase passenger train speeds by lowering the center of gravity on passenger cars. Montreal Locomotive Works (and successor Bombardier) developed the LRC train in the 1970s (LRC being an acronym for Light, Rapid, Comfortable). While tested (and rejected) by Amtrak for use in the United States, the trainsets became the backbone of VIA Rail's Windsor–Quebec City corridor in Canada.

Above: The LRC trainsets originally had their own low-slung locomotive to provide power, but after two decades of service the locomotives were retired. The LRC cars remained in service, however, powered by conventional motive power. In addition to the lower center of gravity, the cars also have tilt technology, offsetting some effects of centrifugal force in curves.

Left: Amtrak's low-center-of-gravity entry has been the Spanish-designed Talgo trainsets. Featuring passive tilt technology, the cars are articulated—adjacent cars share a single axle at each end. The Talgo trainsets have been used exclusively on Amtrak's Cascade service in Washington and Oregon. Motive power is specially painted (but otherwise standard) Amtrak locomotives.

Above: The most modern commuter coaches in the United States entered service on New Jersey Transit in 2006. These 201 coaches and 33 cab cars were built by Bombardier. Platform length is the limiting factor for capacity, so putting more seats into the same number of coaches is the challenge. The design of the Bombardier cars allow for more capacity without making trains longer.

Opposite top: The Chicago, Burlington & Quincy introduced the "gallery" commuter car in 1950 for Chicago commuter service, and other Windy City railroads soon adopted the car style. Gallery cars are bi-levels, with the top level featuring single seats along both sides of the car. There is no floor between the left and right sides on the upper level, allowing the conductor to simply reach up to collect tickets. Commuter railroads in San Francisco and Montreal also purchased new gallery cars, and second-hand cars are used in other cities.

Opposite bottom: The Comet railcar was introduced by Pullman-Standard in 1973 for use on New Jersey commuter railroads. Since then, all cars purchased by New Jersey Transit have had the "Comet" name despite being built by Budd and Bombardier to different designs. The Comet design is also the basis for Amtrak's Horizon fleet and Metro-North's Shoreliner cars.

One of the most successful modern coach designs has been the octagonal commuter car introduced by Canadian builder Hawker Siddeley. First built for GO Transit (Government of Ontario) for use around Toronto in the mid-1970s, the bi-level cars have been purchased by many major commuter agencies in the United States and Canada. Each car can carry about 360 people, and more than 700 cars have been constructed.

Left: One variant of the Hawker Siddeley bi-level is the cab car, designed to lead trains. The cars sport a complete operating cab and are connected to the locomotive (which provides propulsion) via internal cables running the length of the train. With a locomotive on one end and a cab car on the other, there is no need to turn a train at a terminal. This saves time and real estate costs, as turning loops are unnecessary.

Above: Although originally designed for Toronto, bi-level cab cars (now mostly built by Hawker Siddeley successor Bombardier) have found homes in far different climates. In the desert of New Mexico, the RailRunner employs the cars on its run north and south of Albuquerque. The RailRunner sports one of the more unusual paint schemes on a North American commuter system, with large roadrunners adorning the cars and locomotives.

Chapter 11

Dining Cars

Dining Cars

At the beginning of the 1860s, long-distance trains were becoming more attractive to travelers. The Pullman Company had introduced sleeping cars, eliminating the need for overnight stops at hotels. But sleep wasn't the long-distance traveler's only necessity. Food was even more important. A way to feed passengers had to be developed.

Early train travel consisted of passengers disembarking for food, usually at a trackside dining room in towns where steam locomotives were serviced. While the locomotive received water and lubrication (and occasionally coal), patrons rushed off the train and into the station for a quick meal. (Historians will recall that it was during one of these meal stops, at Big Shanty, Georgia, that James J. Andrews and his raiders stole the locomotive *General* and initiated the Civil War's "Great Locomotive Chase" in 1863). In the Northeast, the first rudimentary onboard food service appeared in 1862, consisting of a car outfitted with a lunch counter where food was reheated and served (not unlike some Amtrak snack

counters today, except microwave ovens have replaced steam ovens).

George Pullman pioneered modern rail dining services, first by incorporating a small galley in sleeping cars in 1867. Porters would take food orders, then return with the food, which was eaten from a small portable table at the passengers' seats. In 1869, Pullman introduced the first traditional dining car, complete with a kitchen and tables. Dining cars made sense for Pullman in attracting and keeping the upper class happy during train trips.

The railroads, on the other hand, were not eager to take on dining-car services, as the high staffing and stocking costs meant most of these cars operated at a loss. Nonetheless, it came down to a matter of economics. To attract passengers, you needed to provide reasonably priced food. The railroads begrudgingly provided dining services, but always have looked for ways to cut costs. Some railroads experimented with snack counters, others with automats.

Dining car layout is fairly straightforward. Most cars have a kitchen and pantry at one end. These kitchens are a marvel unto themselves. Here, staff can prepare any five-star meal that a restaurant kitchen can produce, but in a small percentage of the space. Dinner trains have become big business in recent times, and many have recruited chefs who have been more than a little surprised at how little space is provided in a dining car kitchen.

It's not just the preparation area that needs to be squeezed into a tight space. Throw in the pantry, refrigerator, and freezer (and remember, you can't exceed the width of a railroad car), and you have some interesting challenges.

The kitchen usually occupies about a quarter to a third of the dining car, with the rest left to seating. On both sides of a center aisle, most cars have tables that can seat four, although some cars have tables for two on one side of the aisle. One pleasure of traveling by train, even today, is that a single traveler or a couple is often seated with a complete stranger. Conversation seems to flow freely while watching the scenery roll past, and more than one new and lasting friendship has been made over a dining car meal.

Dining cars never have been the most economical way to feed a traveler, and railroads have always searched for ways to contain costs. Even today, Amtrak struggles to balance the cost of service against the cost to the passenger (in just about every instance it costs more to prepare the meal than what a passenger is willing to pay, so operating at a loss is usually standard). Amtrak solutions have included everything from standardized menus on every train in the country to elimination of all onboard cooking (serving reheated, pre-cooked meals instead). Nonetheless, Amtrak's employees have been resourceful, and their dining car chefs have been particularly proud of their work. Even with the most draconian budget cuts there always seems to be a way to keep the dining car experience at a high level. Most recently, the trend has been to give up on cutting corners. Most Amtrak trains have food prepared to order from regional menus. The dining car remains a lasting example of classic train travel.

Previous pages: Even though passenger trains attract fewer riders today than they did in the early twentieth century, the dining-car experience still remains a part of Americana. Dinner train operations have sprung up all over North America, featuring everything from pizza parties to five-star meals. The Napa Valley Wine Train has been operating dining-car service since 1989.

Above: Fine dining has always been a part of long-distance passenger travel. The Atlantic Coast Line offered dining-car service on its *Champion* between New York City and Florida. Competing Seaboard Air Line also offered premium service on its *Silver Star* and *Silver Meteor,* competing with ACL's service.

Opposite bottom: Alaska is a growing market for rail passenger service, primarily for sightseeing. The major cruise lines, including Princess, Royal Caribbean, and Holland America, have all entered the Alaska market, utilizing combination dome/diners. Most of the cars in Alaska service were rebuilt from 1950s-era cars, but some are new.

Above: The Philadelphia & Reading's *Lee E. Brenner* is a classic heavyweight diner that still sees regular service on the Strasburg Rail Road in Pennsylvania. The steel car still serves its intended purpose, with its wait staff offering fine meals as the Amish Country scenery rolls by outside the windows.

Right: It's time for dinner in the diner, a tradition of the great passenger trains. Fine china, fresh-cut flowers, and linen tablecloths were always present, and you could usually count on making new friends at your table as a courteous wait staff met your every need.

Above: VIA Rail's Budd-built dome cars are actually dome/diners. Each car has table seating for 24 in the lower level, with another 24 seats located in the dome. Each car also features a lounge and a coffee shop. The Skyline domes were constructed in 1954 and 1955 for Canadian Pacific; of the 18 built, VIA still operates 16.

A dining-car chef not only had to be talented with cooking, but he had to make do with cramped quarters and contend with a bouncing train. Still, during the golden age of passenger trains, dining-car meals were often some of the best food that could be found anywhere—even including grounded restaurants.

Chapter 12
Sleepers

Sleepers

Long-distance rail travel wasn't always the (nearly) nonstop experience that became the norm in the twentieth century. Today, only a few station stops interrupt a passenger's progression to his or her destination. But when railroad travel first developed, trains would stop at trackside rest areas for meals and at posh hotels for the night.

Business travelers demanded faster service from the railroads, however, and the most time-consuming part of the long-distance journey—staying at hotels each night—needed to be eliminated. The first sleeping cars, or "sleepers," appeared in the 1850s and were privately built and operated. These early cars served as fancy parlor cars during the day, with seating that could be converted to sleeping space for the night. By 1870, the company founded by George M. Pullman, whose name became synonymous with luxury rail travel, was the premier sleeping-car builder and operator.

In 1865, Pullman built a car named the *Pioneer* that became the standard for all sleepers to follow. It introduced the "open berth," a bed that ran parallel to a car's center aisle and used heavy curtains to keep out light and noise. Open berths were stacked ("upper" and "lower"), with the lower berth usually made from the conversion of two daytime-use seats, while the upper berth folded out from the wall. Soon, Pullman was cranking out 12-1 cars (1 drawing room and 12 open sections, each section having an upper and lower berth) that were the typical sleepers into the 1930s.

Most of today's overnight travelers on Amtrak have only ever experienced sleeping cars with private rooms (some trains operated by VIA Rail in Canada still have open sections). This is a relatively new configuration, however. Pullman didn't manufacture the first private-room cars until 1927, and then only for the use of the very wealthy. While a 12-1 sleeper could accommodate more than two dozen passengers, single-room cars could usually accommodate only about a dozen people. Since only the wealthy could afford space in a single-room car, the rooms were furnished in a posh manner.

Nonetheless, even folks of lesser means wanted more privacy and space than could be afforded by an open section, so Pullman created sleeping cars for the not-quite-as-rich. These cars appeared in a variety of configurations. Most were a combination of open sections and private rooms. The double-sleeper put two people into each room, further maximizing the potential revenue. An economy sleeper that featured 16 single (although small) rooms in a staggered semi-double level configuration remained quite popular into the Amtrak era (where they were known as Slumbercoaches).

Sleepers could become uncomfortable (and potentially odoriferous) places on hot nights. Open windows let in too much noise and closed windows kept in too much air. In 1927, Pullman created the first air conditioning for passenger train applications and the idea spread quickly. Early air-cooling systems usually used ice or mechanical means to cool the car, with air circulated by fans. Soon, air conditioning use expanded from sleeping cars to the rest of the train, and most passenger cars built in the streamlined era featured sealed windows.

In the years following World War II, Pullman created yet another sleeping car that became the de facto standard: the 10-6 sleeper. These cars featured a Pullman room design called the "roomette," which featured a bed hidden in the wall during the day and a hidden toilet/sink combination. Ten roomettes were combined with six double bedrooms in each car, hence the 10-6 designation. All-roomette cars could have up to 18 rooms.

Today's Amtrak passengers are treated to private rooms on most long-distance trains, which typically use Superliner cars. While Superliners are used for just about everything from coach to diner to lounge, they are particularly well-suited for use as sleeping cars. The Superliner's bi-level configuration allows for private rooms on the upper level, while the lower level can be used for baggage, a family sleeping room that can hold up to five, or additional coach seating space.

In Canada, passengers can be treated to a traditional sleeping car experience on VIA Rail, particularly on the long-distance *Canadian*. This train, composed entirely of Budd-built stainless-steel cars from the mid-twentieth-century, has private rooms (some in the classic observation car/sleeping car combination that trails the train) and open sections.

Previous pages: VIA's Chateau- and Manor-class sleepers are part of the consist of the *Canadian* as the train makes a three-day trek from Toronto to Vancouver. The Chateau sleepers feature three sections, eight roomettes, one drawing room, and three double bedrooms. The Manor class has three sections, four roomettes, one compartment, and five double bedrooms.

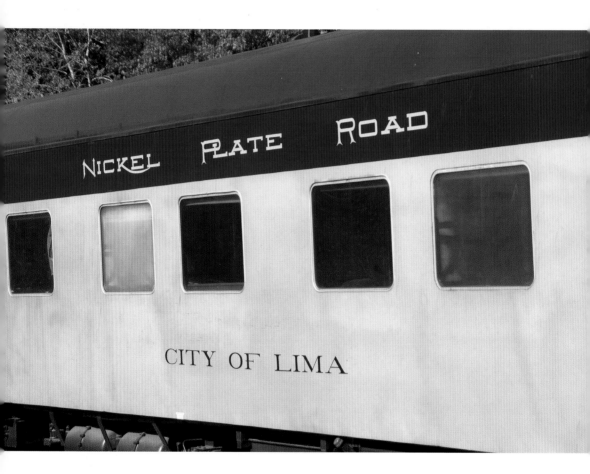

Nickel Plate 211, the *City of Lima,* was built in 1950 by Pullman-Standard. The car features 10 roomettes and 6 bedrooms, thus the designation "10-6 sleeper," a common configuration. It served the Nickel Plate until 1963 and later was used by the Illinois Central and Chicago & North Western. It has since been restored to its Nickel Plate identity.

Above: The *Cabot Manor* is a stainless-steel product of Budd. The car features three sections (which include an upper and lower berth; think of Marilyn Monroe's *Some Like It Hot*), four roomettes (small bedrooms for one or two people), five double bedrooms (with toilet and shower), and a compartment (a spacious room by railroad standards).

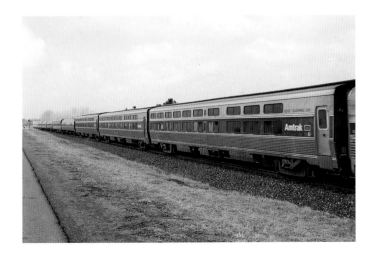

Left: The Viewliner is Amtrak's modern single-level sleeping car, built by Morrison-Knudson in the mid-1990s. Each car has a dozen roomettes, three bedrooms, and one handicap bedroom. Unlike most sleepers, the Viewliners have a small row of windows along the top of the car, which gives the person in the top bunk an outside view.

The typical Superliner sleeper room isn't much different from sleeping cars of previous eras. Two facing seats next to the window fold down into the lower berth, while the upper berth folds down from the ceiling. Amtrak attendants still fulfill the historic duties of the porter, making up the beds each evening and returning the room to day use while the passengers are at breakfast.

Left: The Superliner comes in various configurations, including sleepers. Externally, it's difficult to distinguish a Superliner sleeper from a Superliner coach. The most common configuration for a Superliner sleeper features 5 bedrooms and 10 roomettes on the upper level, and 4 roomettes, a family bedroom, and an accessible bedroom on the lower level.

Above: A Superliner-equipped train makes its way across the Nevada desert, heading for the warm sunshine of California. The car with the glass in the roof is a parlor car; the remaining cars are coaches, sleepers, and a diner. A Superliner sleeper was the last car built by the great Pullman Company, rolling out of the plant in July 1981; it was named in honor of George M. Pullman.

Chapter 13

Observation, Parlor, and Business Cars

Observation, Parlor, and Business Cars

The rich and powerful once rode the rails with style. Picture a rail baron riding on the rear platform of an open observation car, sitting back in his chair, feet propped up on the railing with cigar smoke drifting back along the receding tracks.

Most passengers have to be content with the limited views. In a coach you can see out either side; in a sleeper you may only be able to see out one side. You can seldom look ahead or behind. The only places to get views like that are on the front of the train (where the locomotive crew has the exclusive view) or from the rear. The view from the back platform is often reserved for the highest-paying passengers or businessmen showing prospective shippers what the railroad can offer.

Observation cars brought up the ends of most premium trains during the heavyweight era (roughly prior to World War II). Usually, the observation car featured sleeper rooms in the forward half, with the back half devoted to a lounge appointed with plush chairs. Some cars were enclosed with large rearward-facing windows and oversized side windows, but the classic observation car had a rear platform where only a brass railing separated the rider from the roadbed. While generically referred to as observation cars, they were more precisely called by all the components each contained, such as a sleeper-lounge-observation car.

Parlor cars differed from observation cars in that they were made for the middle of the train, with standard vestibules at each end. The clientele, however, was the same. Parlor cars were first introduced by the Pullman Company as the daytime companions to sleeping cars. Parlor cars had single seats on each side of the aisle, with attendants waiting on each passenger's needs. Seating was plush and décor was lavish.

In 1933 the Pullman Company introduced a streamlined car named after the company's founder, George M. Pullman. This lightweight car pioneered the vast change in passenger equipment that was to come. At the rear was a lounge area, but rather than an open platform, the car was tapered, making it the first of the "boat-tailed" observation cars. This design eventually trailed the semi-permanently coupled lightweight *Zephyr* trainsets that ushered in streamlining and dieselization.

Many railroads had their own style of enclosed observation car. The New York Central's *20th Century Limited* and the Pennsylvania's *Broadway Limited* both had observation cars with somewhat flat rears. The Milwaukee Road had its famous Skytop lounge cars shaped like a beaver tail, with glass panels in the ceiling. The *California Zephyr* had a more traditional boat-tail car. In Canada, VIA's *Canadian* still boasts a boat-tail sleeper–lounge–dome observation car.

The close cousin of the observation car is the business car. In fact, the only difference might be in the cars' occupants. Business cars have served two functions: getting the railroad's officials from town to town (a practice since replaced by private jets) and entertaining current and prospective customers (shippers). What better way to show a client your railroad's assets than from the back of the train, where every siding and freight facility can be seen?

The business car is still a vital tool for most railroads, but the standard rear-platform car has been replaced by the theater car. Theater cars have one large floor-to-ceiling window at the rear (protected by a roll-down door when the car is not in use) and rows of seats facing the tracks, with each row slightly higher than the row before it. Since most railroads don't operate their own passenger trains (that duty was passed on to Amtrak in the United States and VIA Rail in Canada), the business car has grown into the business train, with sleeping and dining cars joining the theater car.

Amtrak does not operate observation cars, although various experiments in luxury service have come and gone. Most long-distance trains feature lounge cars, open to all passengers, with some table seating and a snack counter. There has been some opportunity to revive parlor cars by upgrading lounge car seating and food service, and restricting access to passengers with sleeper accommodations. Private operators such as GrandLuxe Rail Journeys offer "land cruises," running entire trains of luxury parlor cars, sleepers, and diners over the most scenic lines in North America.

Even though parlor and observation cars have almost vanished from passenger trains, the survivors still carry out the same function as their nineteenth-century counterparts: provide the finest luxury rail travel to the most discerning clientele.

Previous pages: No first-class passenger train of the mid-twentieth century would be complete without an observation car, such as those found on the Southern Pacific. It was here that the rich and the famous sat and watched the railroad recede, all from the comfort of a glass-surrounded lounge. Other observation cars were used by the railroad's president or even privately owned by the most elite.

Right: The classic railroad observation car featured an open rear platform for unobstructed viewing of the right-of-way. Upper-class businessmen and railroad officials in the early twentieth century spent many an hour enjoying a cigar while watching the tracks recede. No open-platform observation cars remain in use on either Amtrak or VIA.

Above: The Illinois Central's orange and chocolate colors adorned trains like the *Panama Limited* and *City of New Orleans*. Open-platform cars were a product of the heavyweight era, riding on three-axle trucks and often built by Pullman. Open platforms vanished in the streamliner era of the 1940s and 1950s, replaced by enclosed lounges.

A large lounge was usually adjacent to the open platform, with large windows and a bar nearby. Most cars of this type had some sleeping space, and observation cars used for railroad business also usually had a dining area. The lounge of Pennsylvania Railroad No. 120 carried the casket of Senator Robert F. Kennedy in 1968.

VIA Rail still uses a round-end observation car on the rear of its premier train, the *Canadian*. The series of cars (actually each is configured as an observation-dome-sleeper car) is known as the Park series, with each car bearing the name of a Canadian provincial park. The cars were built by the Budd Company in Philadelphia in the mid-1950s.

Above: When the Milwaukee Road reequipped its *Morning Hiawatha* and *Afternoon Hiawatha* trains in 1948, it placed distinctive homebuilt Skytop lounge cars at the rear. Featuring windows curving up to the ceiling, the cars were heralded as art deco masterpieces.

Left: The *St. Lucie Sound* was built by the Budd Company in the 1950s for the Florida East Coast Railway. It featured two lounges and the classic boat-tail configuration. Similar to Canadian Pacific's Budd-built Park cars, the *St. Lucie Sound* lacked a dome and sleeper space.

Right: In modern railroading, the theater car has become popular on business trains operated for railroad officials. Featuring a large single rear window, the cars also have several rows of inclining seats, much like a theater. The rear window is protected by a roll-down cover when the car is not in use.

Above: The rear of a typical observation car usually features a lounge with comfortable seating and tables. Often, the car also has a bar or small kitchen, while the forward portion sometimes features a dining area, second lounge, or sleeping space. Observation cars are not found on Amtrak, but operators such as VIA and ON Rail in Canada still use them.

Many private cars remain in service in the United States, owned by groups or individuals and operated behind regular Amtrak trains. Naturally, one of the most popular types of private cars is the observation car, taking full advantage of back-of-the-train positioning. Often, a private observation car is accompanied by a private sleeper (as seen here) for overnight trips.

Chapter 14

Cabooses

Cabooses

For 120 years the typical freight train was trailed by a caboose—a red caboose, if you subscribe to tradition. Ironically, the caboose produced the least revenue of any car in a freight train, yet it is the most familiar car to the general public.

Every train requires many people to operate it. This was especially true in the early days of railroading. In addition to the engineer and fireman, each train had a conductor—the real "boss" of the train. Even though the engineer controlled the locomotive, no movement could be made without the permission of the conductor. Each train also had one or more brakemen. In the early days of railroading, most trains were "mixed"; a locomotive would haul a combination of passenger and freight cars. Thus, the conductor and brakemen could simply ride in one of the passenger cars. But as freight-only trains became more common, crewmembers other than engineers and firemen needed a place to ride (steam locomotive cabs were usually small and cramped). Often, a boxcar was employed for this service, and in the

1840s boxcars exclusively for crew use began to appear. These had smaller side doors to replace the large cargo doors. Crews further modified these boxcars by adding comforts such as a desk, seats, a stove, and rudimentary bunks. The first true cabooses, incorporating all these comforts as standard equipment, appeared in the 1860s.

The caboose served many functions. It was a rolling office for the conductor, with a desk for him to complete his paperwork. And when crews made long trips from their home terminal, the caboose served as a hotel room, equipped with bunks, a toilet, and a stove for warmth and meal preparation. Since crewmen had to perform such duties as throwing switches and protecting the rear of the train from following trains while stopped, the most convenient position for the caboose was at the back of the train.

As they became more functional, cabooses started to look less like boxcars. Side doors were replaced by end doors leading to a platform from which the crew could observe the train and the railroad. A cupola was added to provide a high lookout to observe their train as it rounded curves as well as other trains they passed on sidings or double track. Starting in the 1940s some railroads replaced the cupola with side bay windows, as increased freight car height made the cupola somewhat impractical for observation. Bay-window cabooses also eliminated the potential hazard of crewmembers falling from the cupola, especially from slack action when a long train was starting. Some caboose manufacturers combined the wide view of the bay window with the height of the cupola, resulting in the "wide vision" caboose.

Early cabooses had four wheels, but it soon became apparent that eight wheels provided a better ride. But railroads weren't overly concerned with crew comfort, so four-wheel cabooses remained common until the early 1900s (laws soon mandated that cabooses have eight wheels). Cabooses were also built with steel underframes from the earliest days, as even then it was common for railroads to use locomotives on the rear of a freight to help push trains on steep grades—a crushed wooden-frame caboose would be bad for the crew and the train's schedule! As with freight cars, all-steel construction became the norm for cabooses.

By the 1980s cabooses were becoming redundant. Modern diesel locomotives had large cabs that could accommodate the entire crew, modern signaling eliminated the need to protect the rear of a stopped train, and automatic switches controlled by a dispatcher miles away replaced the need to manually throw siding switches behind the train. But the real death blow to the caboose was the development of the "end-of-train" device (EOT). More commonly called a FRED (flashing rear-end device), these boxes are mounted to the rear coupler of a freight train and deliver telemetry to the cab. Important information such as the air pressure in the brake system at the rear of the train can be monitored by the head-end crew. Two U.S. states passed laws mandating caboose use for safety reasons, thus keeping the caboose on main lines for a couple of extra years, but eventually these laws were eliminated. Shortly thereafter, the Canadian regulations did likewise. By the 1990s, the last cabooses were used only on branch lines and in work-train service.

Previous pages: The red caboose is probably the most recognized piece of rolling stock. Like the steam locomotive, cabooses have all but vanished from the rails, a victim of economy and technology. But today, two decades after the end of most "cabin car" operations, ask anyone what is found at the end of the train and they'll still say the red caboose.

Wood construction and red paint made for a fairly typical caboose throughout the first half of the twentieth century. While the caboose was of wood construction, the frame was made of steel to withstand the rigors of riding behind a freight train. A long freight train would have a lot of slack between the cars when stopped, and when a freight started up, the locomotive could be moving at a fairly brisk pace before the caboose was jerked into motion at the rear. "Hang on" was the rule for riding in the back.

Left: This Illinois Central caboose, built in the railroad's own shop in 1941, was fairly typical with one exception: it had a high side door in the middle. This door was used for loading small less-than-carload parcels on lines that otherwise didn't offer express package services. Sometimes perishables were loaded into the caboose to be stored in a large refrigerator.

Above: Sometimes caboose construction was fairly simple. Many railroads, such as the Soo Line, simply used plywood sheathing for caboose sides. Because cabooses were not revenue-generating cars (unlike most other cars on a freight), some railroads simply didn't invest money in their upkeep. Crew comfort was not a high priority for some railroads.

Above: Early cabooses had only two axles and were known as "bobbers." Since cabooses didn't generate any revenue, the idea was to keep them as light as possible. Four-wheel cabooses were certainly light, but were notoriously rough-riding. State laws enacted in the early twentieth century dictated a minimum caboose length or mandated two two-axle trucks. The last bobbers were built around 1921.

Opposite top: Despite their customary position at the rear of the train, cabooses had to get sturdier as locomotives got more powerful and trains became larger. The reason? In mountainous terrain there was often a "helper district" where locomotives were added to a consist to assist a train over a grade. The customary spot to place this extra power was at the rear of the train, behind the caboose. Imagine being a conductor, with a large steam locomotive pushing just a few feet from your desk.

Opposite bottom: While red is considered the traditional caboose color, you could find cabooses in almost any color. Many industrial railroads used yellow, primarily for visibility. Kennecott Copper was one such industrial road, using yellow cabooses on its mining operations in Nevada.

Since one of the primary purposes of the caboose was to provide a place for crewmen to keep an eye out for defective equipment while the train was in motion, different means were developed to increase visibility. One of these developments, which caught on in the 1960s, was the wide-vision caboose. A standard cupola was widened to put the watching crewman further out from the side of the train, making it easier to spot defects on tangent track.

Above: Another development to aid visibility was the bay window caboose. Like the wide-vision caboose, it put the crewmen further out on the side of a freight to increase visibility. One big advantage the bay window caboose had over cupola-equipped cabooses was the elimination of dangerous ladders, thus minimizing falls during severe slack action.

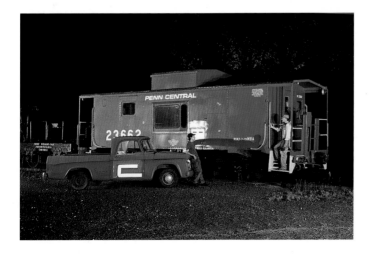

Left: Some railroads modified standard cabooses into bay window models in the 1960s and 1970s. Sometimes the cupola was retained, although the windows were blanked out and ladders were removed. Overall, the result was a safer caboose with better visibility, though the cars' aesthetics could be questionable.

Right: The cupola provided an elevated perch from which to watch the train for defects. A common problem for freight trains before the advent of roller-bearing wheels was the "hot box." Oil-soaked rags placed in journal boxes would dry out and the journals would overheat. It was up to the caboose crew to spot telltale smoke rising from the wheels before an axle failed.

Above: The caboose was also a rolling office for the train's conductor. Tables, and often a desk, were provided. Paperwork on all the cars delivered or picked up by a freight train had to be filled out, and the conductor had to ensure that each car arrived at its proper destination.

Cabooses were often assigned to a particular crew; each time a crew went out they took their "own" caboose. When a roundtrip resulted in an overnight stay at an outlying terminal, the crew stayed on the caboose. Tables provided a place to eat, and often a newspaper served as a simple tablecloth. Bunks were also provided for overnight stays.

INDEX

192